Stress Free Directing

Strategies for staging a play or musical for the director who has a day job and wants to keep it

Daniel B. Mills

copyright 2015 by Daniel B. Mills

Contents

Introduction

Chapter
1. Directing is Fun: *If Rehearsal is Fun for Everyone*

2. Principles of Composition: *Beauty and Focus*

3. Development of Free Blocking

4. Advantages of Free Blocking

5. Principles of Free Blocking

6. Where Actors Move: *Stage Positions*

7. How Actors Move: *Conventions of Stage Movement*

8. Why Actors Move: *Motivation*

9. Groups and Tableau: *Beauty in Composition*

10. More Ideas for Stage Movement

11. Sample Scene: *Stress Free Directing in Action*

Introduction

This book is for the stage director of school and community theater.

The first thing I want to know is: Are you crazy?

Crazy helps.

Staging the school play, the school musical, the festival one act, a community theater musical or operetta is a huge undertaking. And you have a day job! So when do you have time to do all the planning it takes to direct an awesome show?

Yikes! Who talked you into this, anyway?

I know, I know. You wanted to do it. You volunteered! You didn't even ask how much they pay their director.

Don't ask. It isn't much.

What did you say? They don't pay anything? Well isn't that just the worst news yet.

No, really, take what you can get, but, if you really need the money, go moonlight in a convenience store. It'll make you more, for fewer hours, and far less stress.

But since you've already committed, and since rehearsals start soon, and you just went on Amazon.com to find ANYTHING that would help, anything with lots of pictures, and lots of practical stuff, and not much theory, it's a good thing you stumbled upon this book.

If that really is the case, skip to the chapters on Free Blocking and look at the pictures.

But if you have the time to read a few hundred pages of awesome ideas, gleaned from years of experience at staging high school, college, community, and professional theater, then please start at the beginning and soak up strategies.

This book is about STRESS FREE directing. (Doesn't it get you all stressed out that I capitalized the words "stress free," almost as if I was yelling at you). Relax, I'm only kidding.

"Stress free" is a fib. I just used that phrase to get you to buy this book.

However, if lower stress, combined with lots of laughter, lots of thanks and praise and hugs, and good reviews, and lifelong friendships is a preferred byproduct of your directing, you are in for a great time.

If you want to stage an awesome looking show without having to re-do everything every time someone shows up at rehearsal who was absent before, you will love this book.

If you want to know how to stage musical numbers without the services of a choreographer... What's that? You have a choreographer? Awesome...that relieves a bit of stress already. But even if you don't have a choreographer, you will love this book.

I do believe that the more you apply the strategies in this book, the less stress you will endure, and the better your show will look.

I love you. I hope you understand that.

Nothing would please me more than you having an awesome show, followed by a letter of thanks to my publisher and a kind review online.

Back to the idea of loving you. I really do. Theater has been my passion, and my avocation for most of my life, starting in high school. I have directed over 200 shows (lost count years ago), and my favorite people are theater people. We have this indescribable connection that only theater people understand. Musicians in an orchestra don't share it. Painters don't share it. Jet pilots don't share it. Neither do bankers, skiers, tennis players, or sports fans. There is something about theater people that makes them special, and I'd rather not try to define it. But you know what I mean.

Maybe mothers have that connection. Maybe. I've never been a mother, so I don't know.

So, because I love you, this book is not about me. It is a gift from me to you. A gift of my life's experience. So it kind of is about me, but it's more about giving you some ideas that will make your theater directing life easier, make your shows more awesome, and will accelerate you into the stratosphere of dazzling show directors.

Ah, but you say, you already know how to direct shows. You've done lots of shows. Acted, directed, danced, sung, and designed. You were selected for this job because you are the best person out there.

Great! The more experience you have the more quickly you will grasp these ideas. You will compare them to your own experience and will morph the whole thing into an even greater set of skills than you already have. In fact, someday you may write a book as well.

But lets talk about this one first.

Stress Free Directing It is a set of strategies for staging a show using "free blocking," a collaborative, artistic method of creating beautiful stage composition that clearly tells the story while encouraging actors to move in response to their character's emotions, and in response to each other. This book is for all of you who want your stage picture to be well composed, the movements to be graceful and economical, and the story to be told with subtlety and power. This book is for you.

I know who you are. I live among you. I direct the same musicals, operettas, and straight plays that you direct. Some of us have written a few original pieces, and some of us have helped students write and perform some plays from their experience and studies. You have chutzpah. You have a wide range of experience in the theater. You believe you can organize large groups of people to pull together a beautiful artistic event. Others believe in you too. You have energy and charisma. You have a way of organizing the rehearsals that is an extension of what you believe works best with people. You could probably play all the roles. You have posters signed by the casts, glowing with sentiments about how they could not have done it without you. We know each other.

You are a lifelong student of the theater.

That's why you are reading this book.

In fact, you probably already have thought a lot of the ideas in this book. Not all of them. But many of them. For we could not be colleagues in this endeavor unless we had developed common vocabulary from the great teachers. You and I have watched lots of professional theater and even more theater by our community and school colleagues. We have copied and modified and reinterpreted what we have seen and enjoyed. We have read esoteric and practical books on directing, acting, and interpreting drama. We have read the critical reviews of plays we loved (and plays we directed), and we have integrated some of those critiques into our own work.

Some of us have entered our plays into adjudicated competitions, and have welcomed or rejected the punditry of the judges. We defend our own vision and execution because we believe in ourselves. We have to. Directing a play is not a task for the indecisive or wish-washy. Usually our vision and execution works, but sometimes it doesn't; a simple consequence of being creative. We bemoan our small budgets, odd theater spaces, and the peculiarities of our limited talent pool, but we love generating creative solutions to those challenges. We are the creative geniuses of theater.

In all these things, we never stop learning about how to improve the quality of our work.

Often, however, we learn not from books, but from our own experience and solution building. Good books about the practicality of our avocation are rare.

It is my hope that this book will serve to crystallize some ideas that have already been stirring in your head. Ideas that you have begun to form, to work with, or to struggle over. If you are a student of directing, or if you are about to direct your first play, you are lucky to be reading this book now. It will save you hours of stressful preparation and painful do-overs.

I hope you find these ideas to be exciting and that by incorporating them into your directing style that your plays will be all the more beautiful, creative, effective, and enjoyable for you and the actors. And all with reduced stress.

This book is about the task of staging the show. But I think we should be clear that there are many aspects of the theater that it is <u>not</u> about.

This book is not about how to coach your actors in the art of acting.. Oops, shouldn't that be included in a book on directing? Yes, it should. But, you'll have to buy the companion book, *Coaching Pre-Broadway Actors: A Stress Free Guide for Directors Who Have A Day Job.*

This book is not about how to produce a play from beginning to end. Maybe I'll publish one of those someday, but don't count on it. There are many good sources for the big picture of directing a community play, including strategies for selecting a play, casting, scheduling rehearsals, and working with designers, costumers, and set builders. One good source is the American Association of Community Theater at www.aact.org. My favorite book is *The Complete Play Production Handbook* by Carl Allensworth. Another good book is *Let's Put On a Show!: Theatre Production for Novices* by Stewart F. Lane a Broadway producer who nevertheless speaks to the needs of amateur companies. And there are many more; just look at the list from your favorite publisher of plays or Google it.

This book is not about choreography. Although I include some important tips about how to relieve the stress for your choreographer as well. And if you have no choreographer for your musical you need this book.

This book is not about design, painting, and construction.

This book is not about costumes.

This book is not about lighting.

This book is about a new way of directing, a facilitative, inspiring, creative, egalitarian, and fun-loving way of bringing a set of actors through the rehearsal process to the final achievement of a high quality artistic performance. It is for the person who is already thus inclined. It is for the director who has at least begun to question the efficacy of the traditional roles. It is for directors who are naturally interested in the creative genius of others. It is for the director who is actively seeking new ways of directing.

It is not intended to force you to change your personality. Rather, if you are inclined to be a facilitative director, this book will give you ideas and encouragement. If, however, you are disinclined, if you are resistant, or if you are very satisfied with your position as a traditional hard-nosed, dictatorial director, and if you are really good at it, please think long and hard before you attempt to change.

This book is for amateurs, including amateurs who get paid a stipend to direct an amateur show. Amateurs work toward the skill of professionals but with the passion of one who is newly in love with the art form. To us, theater is not a job, a duty, a marriage, a livelihood, or a long run. To us, the performance is short-lived and tight. It is like a lovers crush. Like a whirlwind tour. Like a campfire that roars. It is a rush. The word *amateur* is one we should embrace. To some, *amateur* has devolved into a synonym for shoddy, but we know better. The Latin root for *amateur* is *love*, and in the case of theater, amateurs do theater for the love of it. I am proud to be an amateur theater director, and you should be as well. This book is for you.

Chapter 1

Directing is Fun

If Rehearsal is Fun for Everyone

If you want rehearsals to be low stress, they should be fun. They should be fun for you, and fun for everyone in your cast.

I'll say it again. Rehearsals should be fun. But you don't have to be a funny person, or a joke teller for rehearsals to be fun.

I don't mean they should be a barrel of laughs, although there are times that will happen. I mean that everyone at the rehearsal should be involved in constructing a spectacular show. Their intellect should be put to use. They should have opportunities to lead. They should have opportunities to demonstrate their skills and their knowledge. They should be recognized and appreciated for their efforts. They should have input into the creation of the work of art. Their bodies should be challenged to do difficult things but they should be loved for trying. Healthy interpersonal relationships should be engendered. They should develop friendships. Ultimately they should feel that the act of coming to rehearsal is something they look forward to with anticipation, and look back upon with satisfaction.

That doesn't happen by chance. It is up to the director to assure that rehearsals are rewarding for the participants. This book will teach you a whole set of strategies to make people want to come back to rehearsal, and to help one another have fun.

N.B. The next section is a bit theoretical. It's important, but it's still more like a graduate school lecture. To be frank, I wrote it several years ago, just after I finished my doctoral studies, and there was this whole mindset permeating my lifestyle that one should begin with theory and work toward the practical. I even had citations woven throughout, and a long bibliography at the end of this book. I dropped that stuff in the rewrite, but kept the ideas. So enjoy, if you are so inclined, and skip to later chapters to get to the pictures.

The Director as Teacher

A good director should be a good teacher. I don't mean a good lecturer, for that is an antiquated style of teaching – the expert at the front of the room talking to a bunch of passive listeners. No. Here are some features of the effective teacher that have implications for directing.

1. **Facilitate Rather than Dictate.** Effective directors facilitate by forming questions that help actors think more deeply about their character; by creating forums for design ideas to be expressed and solidified; by leading discussions about meaning; by encouraging and supporting actors as they invent movements and stage positions that tell the story.

2. **Honor Personality Differences.** Good teachers recognize different personality types and different learning styles, and different forms of intelligence, and they structure their lessons so that each of those types of people can find success. Effective directors cast people in roles that suit their strengths; create choreography that is challenging yet doable; and create an atmosphere of acceptance and appreciation among cast and crew while assuring that each voice is heard. Rather than trying to make everyone be like you, honor and appreciate the various ways in which people approach the challenges.

3. **Define your Outcomes.** Know what you want to accomplish before you begin. Good teachers today structure lessons that have clearly defined outcomes, and those outcomes are measured as much by what people do, as by what they claim to know. Effective directors structure rehearsals with clear goals in mind and give training and assignments to the actors that help them reach the rehearsal goals. The ultimate goal is for a show-ready performance of quality worthy of the phrase, "Look out Broadway, here we come."

4. **Connect the Play to the Real World.** Don't waste time on esoteric exercises, rather link each exercise to the rehearsal goal and to lines and scenes in the show. Furthermore, connect the themes of the show to the struggles in our world today.

5. **Teach Your Cast How to Think Like an Artist.** Good teachers teach students how to think and how to learn, and not just what to think and what to learn. Effective directors teach actors how to make their own decisions about movement, spacing, and use of props; teach actors to respond to each other and to the entire stage picture

rather than teaching them to learn prescribed movements as decided by the director.

6. **Facilitate Ownership.** Good teachers look for ways to hook students into learning, to get them interested in the subject so that they are inspired to learn on their own. Effective directors understand that people own their own discoveries, their own ideas and suggestions, and their own solutions to problems. Effective directors challenge actors to figure things out, and to own their acting choices.

7. **Assign Creative Tasks to Teams.** Good teachers ask students to create and complete projects of their own design. Effective directors use small teams led by rotating leadership to create solutions to staging challenges, ranging from creating comedy, to creating whole group choreography.

8. **Rotate Leadership.** Good teachers ask students to incorporate service learning, which means that students should share their learning with the greater community. Effective directors give actors opportunities to lead warmups, training exercises, and scene development teams so that each person is responsible for helping others achieve success.

9. **Collect Knowledge From Your Cast.** Good teachers set up environments where learning-on-your-own is rewarded. Effective directors encourage actors and directors to research, and to share that research in an appreciative environment. Many minds produce better results.

10. **Focus on Performance.** In today's schools, evaluations are based on what students are able to do, and not just on what content knowledge they have memorized. Effective

directors know that the performance is the ultimate test. Being able to talk about a play, intellectually, is valuable, but is not the same as doing it. Effective directors keep the focus on performance.

11. **Coach.** Good teachers are coaches. They know what good performance looks like, and they know how to teach their students how to grow closer and closer to excellence. Effective directors don't disparage the stumbling efforts along the way toward excellence, rather they appreciate the effort, then encourage actors to try it again, with additional side-coaching to refine the performance. Hence actors are given a chance to shoot ahead if they have the skill and motivation, or a chance to recover and re-do if they fall short. Effective directors encourage multiple opportunities to re-do a scene.

12. **Dip Into Your Bag of Tricks.** Good teachers have a variety of exercises at their disposal, exercises that teach, that challenge, that build skills. Effective directors collect exercises from every opportunity –books like this, masters classes, college classes, and other theater experiences. They pull those out of their bag of tricks as the moment demands, when they see actors struggling to grasp concepts, or to accomplish effective characterizations.

13. **Shoot for Greatness.** Good teachers know that students like to test themselves against the standard, especially if they can try it again and again and mark their improvement. Effective directors keep teaching actors what a great performance looks like, by showing models, by demonstrating, by selecting and showing off great moments from the ensemble and by teaching. Rehearsal is all about trying it again, and trying it differently, without fear of disparagement.

14. **Memorize, but also Invent.** Good teachers know that memorization is important, (especially for an actor) but so is invention, experimentation, research, writing, reading, questioning, debating, and conducting oneself with a level of responsibility and dignity. Effective directors demand that actors know their lines and music accurately (memorize), but also they expect actors to invent movements, experiment with emotional responses, research their character, question their character's motives, and deliberate among themselves about things such as meaning, author's purpose, and the most effective ways to communicate those meanings. Directors also model and demand high levels of responsibility and dignity from their cast.

15. **Remind the Cast to Do Their Homework.** Good teachers today recognize that students deserve studio time, personal time, group task time, and time to write and reflect on their own learning. Effective directors ask their cast to do homework, which is not only memorizing their lines and music, but also researching their character. They also provide opportunities for processing (reflective thinking) of training exercises, so that actors internalize the learning opportunities provided by training exercises.

16. **Ask Open Questions.** Good teachers today are adept at asking questions that inspire new ways of thinking. Effective directors ask questions that are open ended, and for which there is no correct or anticipated answer. They ask, "Is there another way we could do this? Is there a way we could use your special talent to take this in a new direction? How can we cross breed these two ideas into something new?

17. **Trust the Creative Process**. Good teachers love it when the learning process goes in a new and unexpected

direction. The effective director encourages a rehearsal process that expands the creative possibilities. Once the show is in rehearsal, it may blossom creatively in directions that had not been anticipated at the beginning. The effective director discusses this creative process with the design team, too, so that surprises are not looked upon as an inconvenience, but rather as inspiration.

18. **Give Feedback Rather than Evaluation.** The traditional concept of grading is a percentage of 100% perfect (which presumes the teacher knows what perfect is). But that is being replaced with a system of providing feedback to the learner, and feedback to the parents and normative data about performance relative to peers as well as to standards. The effective director provides feedback at every rehearsal, to every actor; encourages feedback from fellow actors; and occasional feedback from outside experts, such as guest directors, critics, and community members with special skills who are invited to rehearsals or to serve as resources to the design team.

Think about how you can incorporate these new teaching norms into your directing. This book will include plenty of examples.

The Director as Leader

Good leaders today think big, set goals, and involve the key stakeholders in decisions that affect them. They know that the collective intellect of the members of the organization outstrip the individual intellect of the leader. Good leaders know that a healthy organization has collective interest in the success of the organization. Each member holds some knowledge of what other members know.

The old style of management, where workers were told exactly what to do and how to do it, flourished for awhile in the beginning of the industrial revolution. But these controlling, super-orderly methods of organizing work have been largely replaced in the modern workplace. The Taylor and Weber theories of organizations, known as scientific management (as illustrated in theater in *Pajama Game)* have been discredited as demeaning to the workers. The hierarchical, bureaucratic, industrial models of organizations have lost favor as less productive, less responsive, and less inspirational to the worker. Theories of management are always emerging, but in a post modern design, there is a greater emphasis on self-managed teams, with flexible and evolving tasks, and a flat rather than hierarchical organizational design. In the post-modern organization the emphasis is on continuous improvement, rather than on a set of goals that, once accomplished, will be the operating principles for some time to come.

To use a sports analogy, listen to today's athletes and coaches after a game. Whether they win or lose they talk about what they have learned about their play, and the fact that they have improvements to make. They are on a continuous journey of improvement. The same with theater. Few actors will ever be seen as fully accomplished, but rather as artists on a personal journey of improvement. In 2010 when Sandra Bullock won the Oscar for Best Actress in *The Hurt Locker,* after 20 some years and 30-some movies, her first comment as she accepted the award was addressed to the Academy, "Did I really earn this, or did I just wear y'all down?" In community theater, the director leads just such a collective journey of people continuously improving, doing show after show over a span of years, for the love of the art form and the good feelings they get while working with others who love it too.

In the theater, it is time for a new kind of leadership. Traditional roles are being replaced with a post-modern design that is respectful of the actors, the techies, the directors, and the producers, and that is effective not for it's control but for its shared responsibility.

Be a Post-Modern Leader

Here are some traditional roles and their post-modern counterparts.

Traditional planning is driven by the director, top down, and leads ostensibly to order. The rehearsal schedule is an exercise in control. Start times are rigid. On-set behavior is constricted by rules. The rehearsal schedule is pre-determined. The chorus actors are made to feel as though they are dispensable, like a worker on a production line. Only the star has leverage, and the lesser stars either resent that power, or aspire to it.

In contrast, in the collaborative model planning is horizontal. People are consulted as the schedule is set, or, they set their own rehearsal schedules. The chorus actor is as important as the star, and is treated as an investment in the future of the company. The rehearsal schedule can flex with the creative flow of the participants. Start times are important, but not more important than the quality of the work that is accomplished. On-set behavior is spontaneous and human, and is controlled collectively by the commitment of the actors to accomplishing the highest level of performance. The director reminds them of the goals, and the actors monitor their own behavior. Stars are human. They earn the respect of others through their hard work, dedication, quality of performance, and interpersonal effectiveness.

The traditional organization of the theater is a division of labor, with specialization, routines, and top down control from the department heads. Unions and management define their roles stringently. The professional orchestra breaks for tea at specified times regardless of the significance of the number being rehearsed. Only the electrician can touch the lights or move a dimmer switch. However, in the collaborative model of community theater, work teams are diverse, and the variety of voices is considered an asset rather than a problem. There is energy and creativity that emerges from the chaos of ideas. Efficiency actually increases when there are multiple voices, flexible networks, and permeable boundaries of responsibility. Anyone can pull the curtain open. Many people know how to operate lights. The rehearsal pianist can continue even when the orchestra must break.

Though your theater must have a division of labor, including a costumer, lighting director, sound technician, carpenter, choreographer and designer, consider yourself more as a family than as a factory. In the same way as parents teach their children about their hobbies and professions, and as husband and wife assist one another in their projects, and as children demand parental involvement in their sports and activities, so should a school or community theater encourage cross-pollination, diversification, and flat heirarchy.

Get people involved in as many aspects of the theater as they can handle. The actor who helps build costumes not only reduces the stress on the costumer, but becomes an additional resource, an idea-generating member of the costume team, and a more respectful consumer of the costume product. The set builder who volunteers for a walk-on role as the Sheriff gains a deeper appreciation for rehearsal, for actors, and for the need for sturdy platforms.

Furthermore, in community theater, the relationship may last a life time. A person who joins the company so he or she can sing bass in an operetta may, over the years, become a specialist in lights, or advertising, or or producing, or make-up, or, even directing. Your organization is constantly growing new participants, new specialists, and future leaders. Keep people involved in as many parts of the process as they can handle, and you will all be better off for it.

Affirm Your Actors as they Take Risks

Actors are sensitive people. Even the ones who appear hard and insensitive are still sensitive people with a wall of defenses that keep them from getting hurt. If you want to get effective creativity out of sensitive people, you must affirm them with words of recognition. You must agree that their choices are thoughtful or interesting. You must allow them to find success and competence in your way of directing.

Acting involves personal risk. "Do I try this new idea or not?" Actors try out their ideas with a level of commitment; a decision to yell, a decision to strike, a decision to kiss, a decision to be seductive. It is difficult and tense when a director sees that invention and says off-handed, "No Good." In free blocking the actor makes most of the decisions, and the director affirms. The director coaches and encourages the actor to make even greater commitment to the decisions, with coaching to move stronger, kiss more hesitantly, or strike with instant regret, etc. It is a process of discovery that is filled with affirmation for the creativity of the actor. Are there decisions that are eventually discarded? Of course there are, but seldom are they discarded without an honest test of their effectiveness.
Here are some important principles of affirmation.

1. **Learn actor's names**, and use them. A large cast is no excuse for not knowing everyone by name. (I am terrible at

names, so I have to use strategies, including having a stage manager beside me to remind me of names, but you will find your own way, I'm sure.)

2. **Thank individuals, often**, for their effective choices and, when necessary, correct their ineffective choices without criticizing. Example, I was working with a particularly difficult actor who didn't seem to get it. I asked him to move to a stronger position than anyone else when he delivered his line. He moved downstage, but he then turned directly upstage to look at the person he was talking to. I thanked him for realizing that moving downstage was strong, but I also had to remind that speaking upstage was not strong. Thank for the good. Fix the bad without criticism.

3. Encourage all actors to take responsibility to **share the thanks**. I end most exercises with the directive, "Thank someone, by name, and tell them something they did well."

4. **Offer Applause.** From Blood Sweat and Tears, "Applause Applause, ...I'll sell my soul for a song, Pay the price and carry on." and From the Tony Award winning musical *Applause* with Lyrics by Lee Adams "What is it that we're living for? Applause! Applause! Nothing I know brings on the glow like sweet applause. You think you are through, that nobody cares, and suddenly you hear it starting...applause, applause, applause!" Applause is an affirmation that everyone understands, not only actors, but everyone.

A True Story about the Power of Applause

Indulge me a little story that illustrates the power of applause, even for people who are not into theater. This is a true story about the power of applause to encourage people to take risks.

I was the principal of a high school in central Maine and our school was preparing for the statewide standardized tests given to all 11th graders. I offered to go into several English classes to lead a lesson on writing. My goal was to get students comfortable with going beyond the standard expository answers and to be creative, to use figurative language, images, and stories to illustrate their thesis. I had one hour with a classroom full of students I didn't know well, and who had a natural intimidated relationship with the principal. I wanted to get them so excited about their writing that they would actually stand up in front of the class and read, because I believe students learn quickly when they hear what other students are writing.

The teacher said, "That's impossible." She knew her students. "Get up in front of the class and read? It'll never happen!" said the teacher to me beforehand. "Some of those kids have never read aloud, not once all year. And they would NEVER read their own work aloud." She might as well have finished her prediction with, "Are your crazy?" but she was too polite to go that far.

It was my plan to prove otherwise, because I trusted the power of applause and affirmation. And I did. Within one hour all of the students, even the painfully shy, had joyfully stood before the class, reading their own work. True story. No kidding. Here's how I did it.

The writing assignments were short, no more than 2 minutes, (I use a timer) and they were very specific, so no one had a chance to run out of ideas and everyone could accomplish the goal. I modeled every assignment and I did the assignment along with them, and I asked the teacher to do so too. I stopped them before they could finish writing and asked if anyone wanted to read theirs.

Reading their work aloud was scary. The first time only one or two were willing, and they did so out of a sense of duty, or guts, or pity for their principal. I was prepared that if no one volunteered, I would volunteer to read mine, and I would ask the teacher to read hers. I didn't need to fall back to that position in any of the classes. When the first volunteers did read I said something like, "Wow, that's great," and **I led the entire class in applause for them.** Applause Applause! Then I asked if anyone else was willing, and I had another offer or two, and I immediately followed with leading class applause. There were smiles.

The next assignment was also short, modeled, and I wrote with them. This time when I asked for volunteers to read, I got a few more offers, and **I led applause after every one of them.** I spotted the shy kids and I asked them if they wanted to read, and of course they said, "No" but then I asked if I could read theirs aloud to the class, and they said, "Yes." One girl actually said "No" but she let me read hers silently to myself, after which I offered her thanks and affirmation that I liked it. After I read the shy kids' papers, we all applauded, and they glowed.

Even the teacher offered to read hers, and we applauded.

Kids asked me to read mine, and I reminded them to applaud for me, too, and they did.

Incremental growth was applauded. After the next short assignment I asked for volunteers to read, and got more offers. As soon as the first person began to read, I stopped her and asked, would you please stand as you read, and she was very hesitant, but as soon as she stood up, before she even began to read, I asked everyone to **applaud for her courage.** She glowed, and read her piece standing beside her desk and we applauded. After that, everyone who offered to read was invited to stand, and we applauded them as well. Then, when one of them stood to read I stopped him and said, would you be willing to come down here and stand in front of the class to read? And I immediately led applause for that courage and he walked down front, read his piece, and accepted the applause of his peers.

Using that same strategy, after another writing assignment every student had willingly read aloud, everyone had at least stood beside his or her desk to read, and virtually all of them had come down front to read, each followed with appreciative applause from peers. **They were having fun**. They were motivated to write their best work, because they wanted to read good stuff in front of their peers. They heard some good writing from each other, from their teacher, and from me. Some of the paragraphs were not as good as others, but that didn't matter, because the act of sharing gave them a chance to hear more ideas and try out some better ideas in their next assignment.

At the end of the hour, we talked about the process we had gone through. All of the students agreed that **they had fun**, that they heard some good ideas, and they all promised to use some of those writing strategies in their essays. The teacher enjoyed it too, and hopefully learned that kids will really produce, will take risks, and will enjoy the learning experience if you provide peer to peer affirmation.

True story. **Applause is a magic tool that every director should wield like a pro.**

Organize the Rehearsals

Organize your rehearsals to use time efficiently, to use the strengths of your creative team, and inspire your cast and crew to produce at the highest level. Develop routines that emphasize the elements of facilitative directing that you value. Your cast needs to know that you are in charge without feeling that you are bossy.

Here are some strategies I have used to start on time and to stay on time.

1. Come to each rehearsal with a plan, including what scenes and musical numbers you expect to rehearse. This plan should be one that keeps people busy. If not on stage, they should be doing something in small groups, or reviewing the free-blocking fundamentals, or working on some scene team challenge. (You're thinking, Ouch,! Planning? Planning? Doesn't that take extra time that I don't have? Relax, I will cover those plans later in the book.)

2. If it's a musical rehearsal I begin with a musical warm up, where the first note of the piano is struck at start time. If its a staging rehearsal I start with the words, "Take your own space, " after which we warm up by reviewing the staging strategies I have taught in previous rehearsals.

3. Because as a director I am often very busy just before rehearsal, with many questions coming at me from many people, I may assign a person, or a rotation of people to lead the warm up activity while I attend to those exigent conversations.

4. Have the stage manager call everyone to places at the prescribed time.

5. Begin with a preview of the plans for this rehearsal, including the time line. Ask the stage manager to keep the rehearsal plans on schedule.

6. Ask the stage manager to give ten minute and five minute warnings when a rehearsal activity is about to change.

7. End with some culminating large group activity, such as a run through of the scene we've just rehearsed, a run through of the

opening number or closing number, or a report out from scene teams. Never let people just leave the rehearsal without enjoying some affirming activity.

Cluster Rehearsals

One strategy I use to organize rehearsals for an operetta or a musical is to create a cluster rehearsal schedule. I plan scene rehearsals such that people who have scenes together come to rehearsal at the same time. They are clustered together. That way no one has to stay for an extra two hours waiting for a scene that could have been done out of order and at the beginning of the rehearsal.

A cluster rehearsal schedule takes a bit of planning but its worth it in terms of time saved, not only for you but for the actors. I use cluster rehearsals when I rehearse all day on Saturday. Actor 1 who starts at 9 a.m. May have scenes that stretch from 9 to noon. Actor 2 who arrives at 10a.m. may have scenes that stretch from 10 to noon. Actor 3 may arrive at 11 for a few scenes with actors 1 and 2, but then stays into the afternoon to rehearse a duet with Actor 4 who arrives at noon. Actors 3 and 4 stay through the arrival of actors 5, 6, and 7 at 2. And so forth. As I said, clustering the rehearsal scene according to the actor instead of according to the sequence of the show uses rehearsal time more efficiently. I find this works well with operettas and musicals, not so well with straight plays.

To plan the cluster rehearsal first you (or your stage manager) list all the characters across the top, and all the scenes down the side, and make a matrix. Put an X under the character for every scene they are in. You can easily see who have scenes together for planning the rehearsal schedule. It works well with musicals and operettas. For a straight play, just start at the beginning and work your way through.

Give Away the Directing Role

That is right, I said give away the directing role. Now that's a good way to relieve stress for the director!

I don't mean to forsake your responsibilities. I mean that the effective collaborative director knows how to teach others and trust others to participate in the shaping of the show. Teach others to create tight groupings. Teach your actors to create blocking in response to the emotional needs of their characters. Teach actors to generate comedy. Teach budding young directors to see what you see, to fix what you would fix, and to think deeply about the concepts you hold dear.

Give people the opportunity to fix problems of blocking, to discuss the themes, to share their vision, to teach others what they know about acting, to lead warm-ups, to lead acting activities, to create business, to create dance movements, to teach others certain dance moves, and so forth. Give others the responsibility to help one another. Teach them to do it well, and guide them as they practice it. The net result will be a show that has a creative sparkle greater than you alone could have imagined. After all, what are you after? A show that looks like all your other shows? Or a show that is unique, deeply examined, and spectacular? Take your pick.

Don't worry that you don't have the strategies yet to do all these things, that comes later in the book. But I do want you to think about how easy it would be on you if other people both know how, and wanted to take some of the tasks off your shoulders.

If you give away the directing role, you actually strengthen your position as a leader, a facilitative leader, a person who trusts and is trusted. Your show is stronger. Your cast are more connected. And they have greater respect for you, because you have demonstrated greater respect for them.

Some ways to give away the directing role include, (1) The Dream Team, (2) Sharing the Vision, (2) the Scene Team, and (3) Community Quality Control.

Invite a Dream Team.

Develop your vision collaboratively using a dream team. The first important collaborative exercise for you as a director takes place before you cast the show and before the designers set off to work. Pull together your dream team, a collection of creative, diverse, and respected idea-guys (Think of "guys" as a unisex term, kind of like "actors" is now a unisex term) whose challenge it will be to assist you in developing a cohesive concept for the show, a concept that will influence the designs, the acting style, the setting, and ultimately the message. The more creative you expect to be, the more important this process. A show that is produced as scripted, as originally designed, in the same era as the original may need only a small dream team and a single session. But to move *Romeo and Juliet* into the 21st century may require considerable work by your dream team. How do you handle the language (leave it alone, I hope), the music, the dance, the sword play, the wedding, the drugs from Father Lawrence, the role of the prince who threatens death to anyone who incites a civil brawl? Just the decision about sword play alone will incite considerable discussion. Furthermore, the decisions you make about the setting, costumes, the details of the feuding families, Capulet and Montague, will have the potential of forcing home contemporary themes. For example, if the families are of different races, or if one is Muslim and the other is from the Christian Right, think where the play would go. If Romeo and Juliet are same sex, or if the two families are gangs in New York, say Puerto Rican from the West Side...oops, been done already. Anyway, you get the idea. The dream team has a great challenge to develop a concept that works, that can be held consistently, and that is as true to the original or as divergent from the original as you decide. Here are some processes I have used successfully in organizing my dream team.

(1) **Invite the key player**s, including designers, music director, producer. But, also invite other people you know who you trust for their creativity, their willingness to explore, and their commitment to the mission of the production company. A team of six to a dozen works fine.

(2) **Plan the session**. You are, after all, the leader. Be prepared to take notes, with chart paper, or on a projected laptop, or a smart board. You may assign small groups to take notes as well. Make sure everyone has read the show and is very familiar with the show. No excuses. Know the script and the music before joining the dream team. Since I often direct musicals and operettas, I like to begin by playing the overture on a big surround sound system, just to get us all in the mood of loving the show. And yes, beer or wine or dinner is perfectly acceptable as an incentive. This should be fun. The dream session will be a free flowing swirl of ideas, some of which are absurd, and many of which will be hilarious. Let them flow. Let the laughter roll. This session should be fun.

It is OK to **explore outrageous ideas**. The bad ones will eventually be rejected. The good ones will eventually be weighed against one another. But, since the beginning of the process is a brainstorm, make it a ground rule that no idea is rejected out of hand. No one is allowed to criticize or reject an idea until it has been explored. You see, one bad idea may lead to another, funnier, but worse idea, that leads to another more serious idea, that leads to a funny, possible, yet odd idea, which leads to an "Ahaa" moment when everyone sort of lights up, latches on, and runs with that idea for awhile. Therefore, part of your planning is to set the ground rules of brainstorming.

An even better way, if you have the time, is to brainstorm the ground rules. It's a good way to practice the procedure while doing something meaningful. Get someone to take notes, and ask the team to set the rules. Use consensus to decide on exactly which rules to keep. Some fundamentals of brainstorming are: (a) All ideas are good, because brainstorms are after quantity, not quality, (b) Don't criticize. This is not about deciding who has the best ideas, or who has the most power. (c) Piggy back on other people's ideas. Use phrases like "Yeah, and..." and "..right, and what if..." See why I suggest that your dream team include more people than just your designers and producers? What if producers kibosh every idea with why that can't be done --"We have a limited budget!" and "I won't be a part of such a stupid idea" are negative, brainstorm stoppers. If you have designers or producers who are disinclined to brainstorm, don't leave them out, but do outnumber them with creative folks.

(3) Begin with (a) a guiding question, (b) a description of the process, and (c) how we will know when we are done.

For example:
Guiding Question: What would be a contemporary setting and concept for *Romeo and Juliet* that allows us to keep the original language while addressing issues important to the 21st century?

Our Process: We will use a brainstorming process, followed by a critical analysis of the best ideas, and consensus decision-making to finalize our choices.

Our Outcome: We will know we are done when we have crafted a one-sentence concept for the show that allows our designers to begin work.

Or, for another example, assuming that your producing company wants to do a traditional musical, such as *Guys and Dolls*, true to the original script, but on an extremely limited budget.

***Guiding Question*:** What unifying concept could we use to stage *Guys and Dolls* in a way that is powerful and entertaining, but on an extremely limited budget for sets, costumes, and venue?

Our Process: We will use a brainstorming process to generate ideas. Then we will take each idea and follow it through to see its strengths and shortcomings. Then we will use consensus to finalize out choice. Consensus means that everyone here agrees with or can live with the decision.

Our Outcome: We will know we are done when we have a low budget concept that we all agree feels like a fantastic and memorable way to stage *Guys and Dolls*.

Share the Vision. After the dream team schemes, there comes the time to refine and design. Challenge your designers to produce designs that expand upon the concept. All along the way you are responsible to share your vision with the designers, the producers, and the auditioning actors. When you finally meet with the actors, it is important to share two visions:
(1) a vision of the finished product, and (2) a vision of the collaborative staging process, which includes your vision of the style of leadership and followership that will bring this show to the stage. The collaborative director is a visionary who shares ideas with the actors and techies, who asks them to work together to accomplish something great, something worthwhile, and something that none of them could accomplish alone. Leadership is a function of the personality of the leader, and the willingness to experiment with leadership strategies that honor the followers. The visioning process should not be shortchanged.

(1) **Share a vision of the finished product.** Pull

out the set designs and the costume designs, or describe to them the current state of the design process. Describe how you came to select this particular play, and why it is important for our audience and for us as actors to produce this play at this time. Describe what you feel will be the emotional impact. What moments in the play are you working towards, and how do you expect that to move the audience to tears? Tell them the inspiring things you have envisioned for this play, stressing those things that will require extraordinary effort, and that will be well remembered. Actors want to be remembered. Actors want to know that their efforts will be recognized, and will be well reviewed. They want to be a part of something spectacular. By visioning the finished product, you help them commit to the difficult work of creating a spectacular artistic event.

(2) **Share the vision of the process** as well, that we will work together as a team, that we will be creative, and supportive, and that their voices will be heard, and that their actions will be noted. Describe some of the strategies that will be used to get there, -- strategies from this book, strategies from your own repertoire.

Lay out the rehearsal process from beginning to end. Give them a rehearsal schedule, which helps them self monitor whether we are on target toward the tight production we have committed to. Help them know when you expect them off book, and how you will rehearse in the mean time. Describe the way you plan to begin and end rehearsals, and how you plan to use their time. Describe the relationships you have discussed with the other directors, and any chain-of-command procedures your company subscribes to.

Make sure to include a vision of the role of the director in the post-modern theater organization. Describe your intent, as well as your current progress toward realizing that intent. Even when you are not yet a full-fledged collaborative director it is OK to share that vision, to describe what you hope to do to accomplish the transition, and to describe where you have been coming from, your experience to this point.

Your team will be honored to work with you, rather than against you, as you strive to implement strategies that empower them, or that recognize their strengths. The leader in the post-modern organization offers servant leadership, and asks "What can I do to help you achieve this vision?"

Assign Some Rehearsal Time to Scene Teams

The scene teams rehearse scenes without the director there.

How awesome is that! Oh, it's scary, too, because you don't know what they'll come up with, right?

Right. On the other hand, long before you create scene teams you will have trained them in specific skills they can utilize. Trust me on this. I will get to the details later.

Scene teams are a powerful process for sharing the creative development during rehearsals with other members of the cast. Not all scenes need to be developed by the director or choreographer. Sometimes the facilitative director trusts the actors and others idea-guys to work as a scene team who are charged with developing creative ideas and testing them in the scene.

The scene team is appointed by the director, based on the needs of the scene and the skills of the team members. Appointing a scene team is not the same as relinquishing control, or bowing out. Rather, the director provides:

(1) **Specific Skills** that have already been taught to the full cast, such as "You will focus on Approach/Avoidance to motivate movements" or "You are to do rounds on the umbrella, and work that into the dialogue"

(2) **Place**, such as "You will work in the up left corner of the stage." or "You will work in the lobby"

(3) **Timeline**, such as "You will have 15 minutes;"

(4) **Specified Team Members**, such as "You will rehearse with just the two lovers, as the butler is rehearsing another scene right now. Your idea guy is Cindy;"

(5) **Specific Challenge,** such as, "You will develop hand dance movements for the last chorus that could be taught to the entire cast," or "You will rehearse pages 2 and 3 with lots of movement;"

(6) **Report Out,** or demonstration of their progress, such as In 15 minutes, we will all gather back here and you will show us what you rehearsed," or "At 7:30 I want to see a report out of Cindy's team. At 7:45, I want a demonstration from the rounds on the umbrella, and at 8 pm we will all come back to practice the hand dancing to the final chorus."

Here is how to delegate the creative development of a scene or musical number to a scene team.

(1) **Teach the skill** they are going to apply to their scenes. There will be lots of exercises, later in this book, so don't stress. I will give you those skills. They might be skills of staging, of movement, of acting, of comedy, etc.

(2) **Discuss the scene**, briefly, clarify the objectives, the relationships, and the outcome we need in order for the plot to move forward. However, you might also include those concepts in your challenge to them. You might tell them to clarify the objectives before they begin the scene work. You might also tell

them to work toward a scene climax. Or, if the challenge is for them to work on a musical number, such as a solo or duet you might remind them to balance the stage, and introduce lots of subtext.

(3) **Send the actors and an idea-guy off by themselves** to play with the ideas and develop some routines that are in concert with the lyrics and music. The idea-guy is not a substitute director, not a person who tells them what to do, but is rather an equal participant in the idea-generating component, a questioner, a person to keep the focus on the assignment. The actors may ask the idea guys to watch and give feedback.

(4) Ask them to **come back and show it to the director** at a specified time regardless of how refined it is. The director will **give them guidance**, input, and words of encouragement.

(5) **Send the scene team back** out to continue their creative work. Sometimes the director may appoint a different idea-guy for subsequent work sessions, in keeping with the concept of a free-flowing mix of creative people.

The scene team is also a great way to accomplish more during a limited rehearsal time. One amateur company I directed had a tradition of rehearsing the musical only two nights a week for two hours, and Saturday mornings. An opera company I have been with for 30 years rehearses only one night a week for two hours, and all day Saturday until production week. My high schools rehearsed three or four days a week, after school, and in the evenings, plus Saturdays all day. None of those is adequate time to rehearse a show as completely as I would like. So, I have had to find ways to use our limited time effectively. The scene team multiplies the use of rehearsal time by having many people engaged in meaningful rehearsal, even when the director is occupied.

A True Story of A Scene Team

In *The Music Man* there is a great duet between Harold Hill and Marcellus, "A Sadder but Wiser Girl for Me." Well, let me be a bit more honest. It's not really a *great* duet, in fact it's one of those songs that could easily have been cut and no one would have missed it. Anyway, I did not ask the choreographer to develop any routines for the song because I wanted it to be more homey, more like a conversation between a couple old friends who had reunited, and if it didn't work out, I would just cut the song, no loss of time for anyone.

So, at rehearsal, rather than telling the actors the specific movements that had been worked out in advance by the choreographer, we approached it as a collaborative experience. The rehearsal time was spent as an open, idea generating time. We did rounds on props. (more on that later) We discussed comedy and how the use of props can inspire comedy. We pulled out some working props from backstage and played around creatively with ideas. A bucket on the head to represent the girl. A wheel barrow to roll each other around. A mop to represent the girl. A shovel, a wine bottle, a straw hat. We played with each of those ideas. Time ran out, and we still had not hit upon the prop that was most inspiring, and the premise that we felt would give voice to the lyrics and bounce of the song. So, it became a scene team assignment. I delegated to the actors the responsibility to work as a team, to use the principles we had rehearsed, and to select a prop or set of props to work with, and to develop movements and gags with those props that release the emotional intent of the song.

On their own they selected the prop of a rope, a prop Marcellus was likely to be carrying in his job as a stable hand. They developed routines with the rope, including tugging on it like a tug of war, tossing it like a fishing line, coiling it around each other and winding and unwinding, getting tied up, and so forth. When they brought it back to me it was partially developed, and was fascinating, up to the moment they discarded the rope to sing the song in a standard choreographic fashion. My eye told me they needed to continue working with the prop, and to develop more ideas. So, collaboratively we discussed what else that prop would suggest, and they went off as a scene team to work some more. We could have added another prop, like the bucket, to combine with the rope, but we didn't.

By the next rehearsal they had developed a routine that used the rope for the entire song, ending with a climactic gag of coiling of the rope around Harold Hill. After the applause, when the next dialogue began, Marcellus ran off stage holding his end of the rope, spinning Harold in his wake as the rope unwound. It was a great moment, a memorable song, marked by creative use of the prop, developed entirely by the actors, rather than by the director. The director was responsible for setting the scene, teaching them to use a prop, and practicing rounds on props with the actors, and for sending them off with an assignment to work on it as a team. What an improvement over a choreographed dance with box steps, grapevines, and a shuffle-off-to-buffalo!

Something fascinating would have been developed had they used any other prop, whether it be the mop, the broom, the bucket, a harness, a horse, a wagon wheel, shovel, or a horse blanket. Whatever prop they selected, there would have been ways to creatively release the lyrics and emotions. The point is that directors can create, but they can also assign actors to be the creative ones. It is incumbent upon the collaborative director to inspire, to teach, to assign, and to review the work in development, and to **trust the process of the scene team.**

Help Everyone Be Responsible for Quality Control

To borrow a phrase from industry, we must maintain a high standard of quality control over the product we release to the public. In traditional theater the director is in charge of quality control, and in larger or more formal organizations perhaps the artistic director, who may be above the stage directors, is critical to quality control. After the show enters production, the stage manager is in charge of quality control.

In the collaborative theater, everyone is responsible for quality, as everyone has a stake in the performance of everyone else. Furthermore, it is better to have more eyes and brains watching out for the quality of the show, increasing the likelihood that something important will not be overlooked. It is up to the facilitative director to encourage everyone to provide input, and to create opportunities, and to allow, not stifle, cross pollinating conversations.

In traditional theater, ideas must be passed through the director, through a chain of command. In the collaborative theater, the director provides opportunities for everyone to critique everyone else. In the post modern theater, quality control is everyone's job. Encourage everyone to notice, to suggest, and to put forth the effort to make the product be as professional as possible. Encourage actors to offer ideas to the costumer, and for the costumer to offer ideas to the actor. The chorus actors can ask for assistance from the lead, and vice-versa.

Ah, but you say, this opens up a can of worms, with too many critics, too many directors, and no one being quite sure who the leader is. It is true that people may react or behave immaturely while receiving suggestions from others or while giving suggestions to others, but, that is simply a sign that they are on a learning curve, growing into a new form of shared management;

it is a symptom of their needs. Expect it. Don't belittle it. Don't enable it. Just recognize it for what it is and keep on moving. The traditional leadership model has failed, partially because it protected people from being confronted by their mistakes. The newer leadership paradigm is becoming progressively pervasive in American organizations and amateur actors who live their lives in the work-a-day world will come to your rehearsals expecting, or at least familiar with, a degree of community egalitarianism.

There are six easy ways to assure that everyone has a say in quality control.

1. Teaming.
2. Randomly mixing the personnel on ad hoc teams.
3. Trouble shooting during notes.
4. Establishing ground rules for healthy critique.
5. Switching roles.
6. Pitching in.

Invite Your Cast to Trouble-Shoot During Notes

At notes, ask, "Are there any problems that we need to solve, and what solutions do you suggest?" You will be amazed at the problems your cast is aware of and troubled by, and the simple yet effective solutions they are ready to suggest. Don't ignore this powerful resource. This is especially important during tech week, when there are set changes, and costume changes that are being integrated, as well as crowds of bodies gathered backstage awaiting their entrances.

Does your company rigidly assign tasks to cast members for set changes? Ask them at notes if it is working, or if there is a problem. The cast may have solutions.

Does a certain costume change create anxiety or delay the beginning of a scene? Ask the cast who are involved if there is a better way.

This seems like a simple thing, and it is. But you would be amazed how many theaters and directors do not do it. The dictatorial director operates from a vainglorious mindset, arrogantly overlooking the greatest quality control element at his disposal: the actors and their commitment to the show.

Furthermore, the simple act of asking the actors for their solutions to problems gives them faith that their wisdom will be honored. It cuts down on the back-stage whining and bickering and picky-picky snooty remarks. It cuts down on the resentment. It connects the director to the cast, and builds a relationship that will become important when the pressure rises.

Establish Ground Rules for Healthy Critique

Critiques can be brutal. Here's why.

First, lets get something out in the open, so we can think about it. Plays are a time art. They are finite in length. They are powerful as an art form, and I believe they are by far the most powerful medium to instigate human connection and emotional reactions. They are more powerful than the visual arts, music, literature, or dance. Plays are the ultimate art form, emotionally. That's the good part.

Plays are, however, of short duration. They last a couple hours, they evoke an emotional response, and audiences stand in spontaneous applause, fighting back the tears. But then it is over. The play is gone. After the run, the sets are destroyed, the costumes stored away, and, most of all, the acting is gone. Aside from a treasured poster, some photographs, some reviews, the play has disappeared into the cloud of passing time. Unlike a painting that can be viewed for centuries to come, the play is gone. Unlike a book or poem that can be read by thousands of people for years, the performance of a play is lost in time.

Once a play has been lost in time, there is no way that participants can explain to others how wonderful their production was.

That's the bad part.

Actors try. They quote reviews. They can tell how their high school Tony from *West Side Story* went on to sing on Broadway. They can tell how they were judged in the one act play festival. They can tell stories about how the audience loved the show, and sold out the last three nights, and so forth, but there is no way they can actually show to others how wonderful the experience was of producing a quality show.

So, they do the next best thing, or next worst thing. They act as though no other production comes close to being as good as theirs. In other words, actors become hypercritical of other shows. In some way, that hyper criticism is intended to demonstrate that they know a good show when they see it. Their experience with high quality shows has somehow given them the inside scoop on quality. They are quick to point out the flaws in others, not because the audience sees or notices those flaws, but because pointing out flaws aggrandizes their experience. The net result is that actors are hypercritical, to the extent of being annoying.

Yes, actors are annoying when they hypercriticize other shows. Do you hear that, actors? You are annoying when you criticize other shows!

Ooops. That can be a real problem when you get a whole bunch of actors together, such as in the cast of your show! What is worse, it can be terribly annoying if you give them an opportunity to critique one another. The critiques can be brutal.

On the other hand, a facilitative director wants to establish a community of artists who support one another, and that includes giving advice and criticism to one another. How do you encourage critique without inviting an interpersonal disaster?

You establish ground rules, and you offer love and appreciation. Ground rules for critiques safeguard the emotional, fragile, proud, insecure actor, and prevent the calloused actor from doing damage to your community. Ground rules allow for growth and change without threat. Actors are sensitive people. They can read the unspoken ground rules very quickly, and they know if you mean what you say. Under threat of attack from others, they would rather be silent, or conciliatory, or guarded, or retributive rather than to endure painful criticism. Clarify the ground rules, follow them yourself, and insist that others follow those ground rules too. In fact, after establishing the ground rules, watch closely for the first breach and stifle it immediately. Others will be watching to see if you really mean it. Furthermore you should engage everyone in monitoring and holding each other to the ground rules. A play rehearsal should be a safe place. A very safe place. One easy way is to teach actors to say "ouch" when anyone says something that can be hurtful to or about anyone else. Teach them to be allies to one another. Actors who say "ouch" can easily remind us that everyone deserves tenderness.

Here are some common ground rules. They are only a suggestion. You may establish others, both up front, and in response to what happens in your group. It is also effective to involve the cast in drafting the ground rules.
1. Question rather than criticize. Be careful on this. Some theorists have posited that women believe that a question is a

gentle and non threatening way to address a concern, while men read into a question the subtext that you feel he made the wrong the decision and they become defensive.

2. Provide a positive suggestion for every critique.
3. Offer to help, and mean it.
4. Ask for help, and listen to the suggestions.
5. No bragging about your past performances. (It's OK to brag up the performance of <u>someone else</u> in this cast.)
6. Discuss the deed, not the person.
7. Don't judge; instead use "I" messages. For example, instead of "It didn't work when he shook hands rather than kissing her," try the I message, "I didn't understand why he didn't kiss her because it sure looked like she was ready."

Offer Love and Appreciation

Even more than ground rules, though, if you remind people and model offering love and appreciation, your company will survive, thrive, and accept mutual quality control. If you offer love and appreciation, others will follow. Appreciation is available in unlimited quantities. It is a cup that never empties. The more appreciative things you say, the more you will find it easy to offer appreciation, and the more you will notice things that can be appreciated. And, in fact, you are likely to receive appreciation in return. A cast that lives in a world of appreciation and love will be accepting of assistance, and quality control suggestions from others, regardless of the ground rules you set. Love and appreciation trumps ground rules every time.

The True Story of Jackson, the Backstage Bear.

One time during production week for a community theater company several members of the cast came to me as their director complaining about Jackson, the set crew manager, being mean to people backstage. This was the week we customarily referred to as "Hell Week," when everyone is over-tired, the rehearsals are every night, and tend to run long. One particularly strong-minded informal leader came to me and said that if I didn't tell Jackson to back off, people would be quitting the show.

Uhh, can you say stress?

I went backstage at intermission to talk, but Jackson and his crew were working hard in cramped quarters, and were, quite frankly, too busy for me to talk to them privately at that moment. So I put it off. After rehearsal, at time for notes, the cast sat on the stage while I reviewed the notes. I could feel the tension, and someone promptly, and bitterly brought up the issue of Jackson, so I didn't waste time calling for Jackson. He and his crew were busy setting up for the opening scene, and at my request he appeared on stage, shirt off, soaked in sweat. He was surly, and the tension was palpable.

I was sure that the cast was expecting me to call him out publicly and fuel the war. Instead. I told the cast about the work I had seen him and his crew doing, affirming his contribution to the show, and asked the entire cast to give him a round of applause.

With the exception of a few steaming individuals, the cast joined in the applause. Jackson, dropped his surly demeanor just a bit, and said it's hard work, and said he knows he's been hard on the actors backstage for getting in the way of scene changes. I asked him if there was something we could do as a cast to help him out.

He told the cast that the scene change at intermission was the toughest, and if the cast would stay out of the way until that change is made, he would be happy. I asked the cast if they could agree to that and they said they would. But there were still some sour faces in the cast.

The next night at notes, I called Jackson out again, and led another round of applause for his work, and he in turn praised the cast for helping out backstage during the intermission.

The third night at notes, our final dress rehearsal, I called Jackson out again, but this time he asked me to wait, so he could gather his entire crew, and he brought them out with him, so they could all be honored by the cast in a round of applause. He named each crew member and something they had done that he was most proud of, and the cast applauded them individually. After that, he apologized for how cranky he had been early in the week, and he praised the cast for being so cooperative and appreciative, and he told stories about how members of the cast had been particularly helpful during the most stressful scene changes. Through two expressions of appreciation at notes he had transformed from a cranky bear to an integrated member of the team, with appreciation to give away. Try appreciation rather than confrontation, and watch the positive results ripple through your cast. True story.

Switch Roles

One of the techniques I have found to be fun and enlightening is to have a rehearsal where the chorus actors switch roles with the leads. You will be surprised to see how many creative ideas and inspiring performances there are in those chorus actors who have been watching, singing responsive choruses, and secretly wishing they had a chance to perform that leading role. Or, in community theater, have the kids play the adult roles. Sometimes the kids have memorized every line, and every blocking movement, and can do remarkably well. Generally, though, it is a rehearsal for the fun of it. But, watch out, because there can be some pretty great performance ideas that come out of that rehearsal, some of which will find their way into the show. Another way to switch roles is in scene rehearsal. Just offer to let people switch roles for a moment. It helps actors understand what other actors need from them.

Keep Everyone Informed

In the post modern theater, information is shared with everyone. No one person hoards all the information. As a result, everyone takes responsibility for solving problems, for creating solutions to issues, and for holding each other accountable for getting the job done. The post modern theater trains everyone. The director shares knowledge with everyone, and as a result, there are dozens of creative minds at work in the rehearsals, rather than just one. Bulk email is the best invention for keeping everyone informed between rehearsals.

Randomly Mix Your Teams

In order to build a collaborative community it is essential that people develop trust in and appreciation for one another. The fastest way to do that is to assign them to work together on short projects. Unfortunately, unless you mix them up, people will tend to select the same partners over and over, never really mixing, never getting the cross pollination that makes ideas spurt. Furthermore, some self-selected groups tend to fall into non-productive patterns such as off-topic conversations, passive resistance, "lets let her do all the work while we stand around," complaining about someone else, or re-hashing the same old blocking or gags. Random mixing gets people working together who might not otherwise meet, people with differing ideas, strengths, and perspectives.

Remember, I said to use random mixing on short projects. Keep those projects short, and afterwards, remix the random groups. In every school or community theater there are some people who don't want to work with someone else, for whatever reason, whether it is prejudicial or honest dislike. Too much of that makes for cliques and alliances. Someone always gets left out, and some compassionate person always feels responsible to work with the outcast. If people feel that they are going to be randomly mixed and then stuck with those people they did not chose, they feel resistant to the groupings. If, however, they are randomly mixed, and the project is short, then they are re-mixed, there is no resistance to random mixing of the groups. Therefore, establish early, without saying it, that random mixing is for quick efforts. Later, once people are comfortable with random mixing, the length of the tasks can be extended.

Use Humorous Methods to Randomly Mix Your Teams

Remember I said rehearsals should be fun? A bit of silliness works well, as long as it is purposeful and wastes no time. Here are some ways to mix silly with purpose. The easiest way to randomly mix is to have people count off by the number of groups you need. Need five groups? Count off by fives. While that works just fine, it isn't silly.

But randomly mixing can be a fun activity in itself, so for the fun of it, here are some ways I randomly mix people. I am more likely to use these strategies when I conduct a workshop with people I don't know, when we are not working a script, but rather learning theater skills, but sometimes I dip into this bag of tricks if I want to add some fun to a rehearsal. (1) Use the exercise to create tight groups. (I teach that later in this book)   (2) Ask people to sort themselves according to some random feature such as shoe color, first vowel in their first name, preferred ice cream flavor, month of birth, etc. (3) Line up according to some random feature, such as alphabetical order of last name or height, then count off by numbers. All the ones are a team. The twos are another team, etc.   (4) Select just the captains (like tossing the baseball bat) and they select the rest of the team, one at a time until everyone is selected. I'm sure you can think of lots more ways to randomly mix teams.

I suggest these because they add an element of fun, and, remember, rehearsing a play should be fun. If you want it to really be fun, require them to line up alphabetically, or numerically, by preference, but no one is allowed to speak. Watch how creative they can get.   I stress the fun part especially when working on a heavy drama, because there is a need for levity, and a need for actors to remember that they are working with other joyful people, even though their show may be intense or sad.

Assign Important Tasks to Your Mixed Teams

What are the projects they can work on collaboratively? Try these.

(1)**Rounds on a Prop**   Each team forms a small circle. Give the team a prop, any prop from the show, and each person does something creative with that prop, then passes it to the next person in the circle, round and round, until the ideas get absurd and hilarious.

(2) **Scene teams.**
(3) **Status Work**
(4) **Give and Take**
(5) **Tight Groups**
(6) **Approach/Avoidance**
(7) **Acting Workshops** (from the companion book *Coaching Pre-Broadway Actors*)
(8) **Creating Props.** Sometimes the cast needs to work on creating some mass-production prop, such as crowns, or headdresses, or masks, or clown make-up, etc.
(5) **Review the Choreography**.
(6) **Memorize lines**.
(7) **Velocity:** Practicing line delivery at high rate of speed.
(8) **Historical research** -- dramaturgy.
(9) **Physical warm-ups**.
(10) **Stage Movement**

I like to send the groups, especially scene teams, to separate areas of the same space, preferably the stage. Send a group up left, one down right, one center stage, one in the front of the audience, etc. It is important that they not go far away, that they can see each other out of the corner of their eye (and get inspired by what they see happening in other groups) and that they hear the laughter and energy coming from the other groups. A little noise is OK.

Select Project Leaders Randomly

Some projects need a leader. I prefer that the leadership is rotated randomly as well. I select the leader randomly, as follows: If the random groups are selected by counting off, I will say, the second (or third, or fourth, or first) person with that number is designated as the leader. Or, I say something like, "Do rock-paper-scissors in your group until only one person is left" or "Find the person in your group with the closest birthday to August 20th." I then tell them to send the leader to me. I give instructions only to the leader. It may be a written assignment sheet. It may be a "challenge", or whatever this rehearsal needs right now. The leader then must take those instructions back to the group and assure that the group accomplishes the mission. See how that empowers the leader, even if the leader is the lowest on the pecking order, suddenly he or she is empowered with knowledge that no one else in the group has. The leader is the most knowledgeable one. If anyone has a question about procedures, they must ask their leader to come to me. No skirting the "chain of command", and hence no undermining of the leader. Like Donald Trump in "The Apprentice" I hold the leader responsible for getting good production from his or her team.

Ask for Quick Report-Outs from the Teams

When the task is finished, it is time for the groups to report out to each other, to show their work, to prove their worth, to select their best product. This can be quick, but it is a step that should not be skipped. Bring the groups back to the large group and ask for a report or demonstration. The group leader should at least introduce the report out. Keep it short. This is not about telling the whole story, it is about demonstrating what you accomplished. Select one group at a time, going in numerical order, for a quick demonstration. Depending on the project I usually ask for something like, "Select your two funniest bits, and show them to us," or "Tell us the most dramatic thing you learned about the history of _____", or, "Show us how fast you can deliver your lines," or "Show us your best puppet," or, "Show us your best tight group in 5, 4, 3, 2, 1, Freeze!" Notice I do not ask them to show everything they have done. That is purposeful. I want them to be selective, to identify what was best or most effective. They have just a brief moment to come to consensus on what to show the large group.

Applaud Every Report-Out

For every team presentation, I ask for full group applause. From every team, I ask that they applaud their leader. For every team, I ask that they thank each other, by name, when the activity is finished, and that includes shaking hands, or chest bump, or high five or butt slap or other physical approbation they feel inclined to give one another. Do you see these activities as building a sense of pride in the community of actors? A sense of shared joy? Acceptance? Creativity?

You need to build that camaraderie, because it is like a cup of water that is being constantly filled then drained. Some of the work of rehearsal will be drudgery, exhausting, or emotionally challenging. You can't always drain the cup. Sometimes you have to fill it. Think of the small group randomly mixed projects as filling the cup, both creatively and interpersonally.

Ask Actors to Brag About their Unique Skills

Ask the actors what they have for unique skills; what they can already do well. If I have an actor who can break dance, and can spin like a top on his head, there is a good chance I will find an opportunity to use that skill during a dance scene, or, better yet, during a comic fight scene. Imagine the audience reaction when he takes a blow to the jaw and falls to the ground into a headspin.

If I have an actor who can juggle apples while taking a bite out of one of them, I will find an opportunity to slip that neat and entertaining skill into a meal scene. If I have an actor who can do back bends, or a back flip, or who can do a full split, or who can do the moon walk, there is a likelihood I will find a way to incorporate that skill into a scene.

Of course these routines are far more interesting when they are inserted into a scene where they are least anticipated. To have an actor do a levitation during a magic show is one thing, but to have a levitation during Peer Gynt's monologue about riding his horse off a cliff is surprising and inspiring.

I remember a young actress who was playing an incarcerated insane woman in the drama, *Marat/Sade*. In a particularly grisly moment of tortured mental illness she burst out briefly into a full operatic soprano voice. It left the audience stunned because it was so surprisingly adroit and unanticipated, as if to remind us that many insane people have a past life of great potential and intensity. Later, that same actress performed in a real opera that I was directing, and she was delightful, but her voice was fully anticipated. It is the skill that is out of place that surprises and pleases the most.

Yul Brenner already knew how to roll his stomach muscles before that bit became so popular in *The King and I*. The actors in *Blue Man Group* were already skilled percussionists before they took off their slippers and pounded them on the coils of PVC pipe to make those famous haunting sounds.

If I have an actor who plays a mean jazz saxophone, it may find its way into my show. That's exactly what happened in an improvised show called "Junk Shop Jazz" that we invented for the state one act play festival. The character who tinkered in the junk shop, fixing lawnmowers and salvaging pieces off old appliances eventually found a rusty looking tenor sax. But when his imagination took over, his saxophone began to sing beautifully. Little did the audience know (until he played) that he was the best jazz saxophonist of his age in the state.

How about the one who can balance a chair on his forehead, or who can ride a bicycle across a tight rope or down stairs?

I once had an actor who could play music by popping his fingertips against his throat while opening and closing his mouth to change the pitch. During the bridge of one of his solo songs he stepped to the mic and popped the melody on his throat, and the audience went wild with delight. Who would have anticipated such a bizarre talent.

I've had banjo players, magicians, fencers, acrobats, jugglers, unicyclists, and ATV drivers put their skills into action. Again, it is the unanticipated skill that is most effective. For example, take the talented cyclist I just mentioned. Imagine the play is about a mother and son, and she calls him to dinner. Rather than having him walk in the back door, wouldn't it be more fun if he comes bounding down the stairs on his bicycle. The audience will love him for it.

Remember this, don't try to teach the actor something that you think might work if only the actor had the skill. Rather, begin by asking the actors what skills they already possess, and you find a way to surprise the audience with it. Ask them to show you what they can do, then file that in your creative basket, and look for a way to let it inspire a moment in the show.

True Story of the ATV The ATV driver, by the way, was playing the role of Kenicke in a high school production of *Grease*. What a great moment it was when "Greased Lightning" fired up it's engine in the back of the house, raced down the aisle, up a ramp, and was airborne across the stage! Again, the audience went wild with delight because it was so spectacular and unanticipated. (It was also very dangerous and I would never do it again!)

True Story of the Harp I once had a young actor who could play the Irish folk harp. We did a cutting of Brian Friel's *Translations,* set in an Irish hedge school for the state high school one-act play festival. The folk harp sat on the stage as a decorative set piece and occasionally a character would brush the strings wistfully. But when the dramatic and painful climax arrived, and the British invasion was at the town, and Irish culture was being destroyed, the old character of Jimmy Jack picked up the harp and lovingly began to play. The beautiful music soared through the hall and underscored the final speech, as the last lights faded. It was a powerful moment. That play won its way to the state finals. It always helps to know what skills your actors have that can be woven into the play. By the way, I am proud to say that several years later that same actor, Chandler Williams, had his Broadway debut in the Tony nominated production of, you guessed it, *Translations.*

On a more sophisticated note, there are other talents that are just as rewarding for the performer and the audience without being kooky. For example, in today's rehearsal I noticed a section of a dance that was crying out for a show stopping moment. My choreographer had completed training the amateur and very young dancers in their moves, and the number had a satisfying completeness to it. But I knew that the orchestration for that number was grand and powerful, and I needed more. So rather than demanding that the choreographer dream up something more spectacular, and go back to the drawing board with the already overtaxed (and unreliable) young dancers, I said to the lead actor/dancer, a mature man, "Can you do leaps? Because I feel like this is a moment where we should have dramatic leaps and a flourish to the ending."

"Sure" he said, and he demonstrated some pretty dramatic leaps, spins, and a couple ways of flying into a knee-drop ending. The choreographer and I stood amazed and pleased, hardly even realizing that he had those skills in his arsenal. And almost simultaneously we agreed that certain moves should be kept, and others refined to fit the piece, and within 2 minutes we had a dramatic ending that showcased some fairly high-skilled dance moves that brought the piece to a powerful climax. It was all because we stopped trying to tell everyone what to do, and just asked the actor what skills he could bring to the moment.

Start and End Full Cast Rehearsals with a Team Meeting

Full cast rehearsals begin in earnest during the Pull-Together rehearsals, sometime within the last three weeks before opening. The Pull-Together is when all of the pieces that have been rehearsed separately are put in order, together with basic stage crew work such as opening and closing the curtains, and bringing in key set pieces. It is at pull-together rehearsals that the actors first hear all of the underscore and the pianist/conductor works out cues in relation to dialogue. It is at the first pull-together that I discuss the importance of listening to the orchestral accents. In fact, I think it is wise to discuss orchestral accents, and then to jump right into a moment where orchestral accents speak to the staging of the show, and make adjustments according to those accents. Quite truthfully, many shows have opening numbers that have important orchestral accents, so, starting at the beginning is usually a good place to illustrate responding to accents.

I begin and end all large cast rehearsals with a team meeting, a call for all actors to stand or sit on the stage, and I sit with the directors in the orchestra. This gives an orderly beginning to the rehearsal, even for those people who are not in the opening scene. You don't want those people with later entrances to miss the director's challenge for that rehearsal, nor to miss the announcements and whole-group information that gets handed out at the beginning.

At the end, I like to finish with a large group scene, such as the act finale, or a big production number, so I know that people had reason to wait for the end of the rehearsal and not slip out early. Then I call all actors to the stage again, and I again work from the orchestra. I review the progress we made during that rehearsal, and I select certain performances that have been worthy of praise and I call attention to it and encourage everyone to give additional recognition and applause to that actor or stage hand. A little applause and thanks at the end of rehearsal goes a long way to bringing people back to the next rehearsal with a hopeful attitude.

Avoid being Controlling

I stress that this is a collaborative venture, and it is not the norm for directors. While doing a web search for other directing viewpoints I came across this statement, pulled directly from the class notes of a theater professor. I was unable to determine from the website the author or his/her college, so I regret that I cannot give an accurate attribution. But read it, and listen to the tone of the relationship between director and actor. Do you want to recreate that tone every time you direct a show?

> *"I noticed that in directing classes I speak very cynical about actors as if they are a part of a set. And they are. "Acting properties" -- self-moving objects. As a disclaimer for my directors I say: "Place them, free them to do the acting." Yes, they ask for limitations, they need them to channel their energy, to be focused, to have DIRECTIONS for their emotions. What freedom would there be without directors tyranny? I say: "Look at the dictatorship of the text! The words are chosen and actors have to memorize them. Why? Because it's the best possible combination. [Directors] should know about the war between director and actors. The conflict means that the two have a mutual subject, common territory, something to decide together. Conflict is the essence of drama. Director fights with the playwright too, you know. If you accept this premise, you will avoid endless useless conversations and confrontations on the set. You will be prepared for a battle and you better be ready to win. What is your victory? When actor feels that it's his choice, his discovery, his act. Don't be too*

shy, you selected the text, you cast them, you arranged the set - you came in long before them, you should know what they are struggling with."

Notice his use of terms like *war, conflict, battle, director's tyranny,* and a tone of authoritarian control. In contrast, I say there is no need to continue that old model of directing. Once you have tried the methods of *free blocking* and *collaborative staging* you will find that there is a shared energy, a shared joy between the actors and director that produces a performance much more deeply understood by all the actors than the old way. "Director's tyranny" should be a thing of the past.

Even a benevolent dictator in the director's role should be a thing of the past. The benevolent dictator is nice to the actors, keeps his/her temper, and greets and schmoozes with warmth. But still, this dictator can go through an entire rehearsal season without once asking the actors for their input, or encouraging the actors to create, or delving into meaning and character through open discussion with the actors. Actor choices for movement are stifled. Comedy is created only by the wit of the director (or by stealing bits from previous productions), but never though the collaborative ingenuity of actors To me, that is a sad state, and is neither the most effective, nor the most rewarding.

Rather, it is so much more rewarding, fun, and stress relieving to trust the ingenuity of the actors, to teach them skills, to coach them to implement those skills, and to applaud their efforts.

You can make this play directing adventure be a pleasure for everyone involved, including yourself.

Chapter 2

Principles of Stage Composition: *Beauty and Focus*

You cannot free block a play unless you can pre-block a play. By that I mean you have to know what a well-blocked play looks like. You have to be able to see and appreciate the beauty of a well-composed stage picture. You have to know how to arrange actors on the set in such a way that there is a dynamic to the lines and shapes, a dynamic that conveys tone, that focuses the eye of the audience on the proper place, that speaks of status relationships, that tableaus the tension, that facilitates entrances, exits, and crosses.

The composition must make everyone easily visible to the audience. It must be able to shift focus with subtle changes of position. It must bespeak the formality or informality of the setting, and it must work with the scenery, the levels, the props, to clarify who the characters are and what they are doing. Once you know the principles of composition you can teach them to your actors. But you have to know them so well that you instantly see when the composition has gone awry, so that you can remind actors of their obligation to the stage picture.

If you are accomplished at composition, you will enjoy reading my thoughts and my vocabulary, for you will compare it to your own, and you may add an idea, refine an idea, or combine our ideas into something even greater than either of us would have accomplished alone.

If you are not yet an accomplished sculptor of live humans, then practice these principles, take pictures of your compositions, both staged and candid, and analyze them. I believe that one should be able to take a photograph of a stage at any time and the composition should be effective. It should tell the story. It should reveal emotions. It should tell who is aligned with whom. It should have tableau. It should have depth and height and balance. It should be beautiful. If it is not all of those, then it needs repair.

What is Composition?

Composition is the placing of people on the stage in such a way that their collective arrangement looks balanced, and beautiful and creates focus on the most important character at that moment in the play. Individual faces are visible as needed, and stage movement creates a smooth flow from one composition to the next, allowing balance and focus to change over time.

Composition tells the story by showing relationships, and by shifting as those relationships change. Composition coordinates with lighting, sets, and costume, and creates a visual impact consistent with the tone, the theme, and the style of the play at any one moment.

Composition is created by manipulating the following elements.

1. Stage Position
2. Body Position
3. Symmetry/ Asymmetry
4. Levels
5. Grouping
6. Focus
7. Costumes
8. Lighting Intensity
9. Scenery

Why Concern Ourselves with Composition?

Sometimes, especially in amateur musicals, the composition is terrible. I remember watching a community theater production of Oklahoma somewhere, probably because a neighbor or relative was in the cast. I remember a whole cast of cowboys and midwesterners crowded across the back of the stage, singing their hearts out, "OOOOOK-la-ho-ma where the wind comes sweeping down the plain…" Some soloist sang a bit, but I couldn't see who it was at first, then someone tried to squeeze through the crowd to get to the front to be able to sing or say a line, A few of them moved their arm sideways with crooked 90 degree elbow, like they were sayin "Aw Shucks."

When the soloist finished he backed up to the line of cowboys, but couldn't get back through the crowd to the rear, so this big guy was stuck down front, in front of the little kids. Then finally some nice lady pulled some kids aside and touched him on the shoulder and he got back through the crowd to stand in the rear again, giving a sheepish grin of thanks, completely out of character. They were having a good time. I was glad to see people enjoying making music and their friends paying the price of a pizza to see the show. But OOOOO it lack-ed com-po-si-tion.

The arrangement of people was not balanced, not focused, and not beautiful. Furthermore it did not make for a smooth flow in transition from one composition to the next. It did not show relationships, nor shifting relationships nor tell the story. It didn't even assure that faces were visible. I don't say any of this to disparage the show. I say it to help define composition.

And until we recognize the impact composition has on the play, we are doomed to put on shows like this down-home *Oklahoma.* What is even more sad is that I could have made that scene look beautiful and focused in just a few minutes with that cast. So could the director, if he or she had read this book.

You know when you have seen a beautifully composed show. You can feel it. It feels satisfying. It feels like you have been treated to a visual feast. It feels as though there has been a consistent tone, a graceful flow, an engaging story. Good composition, ultimately, is about bringing the story to the audience in a way that they understand through their visual senses, as will as their auditory senses. When we watch a well-composed show we don't feel as though we missed an important plot point. That's because the director kept us focused on what was important. We noticed the slightest reactions. We noticed the subtext. We noticed, through people's body positions who was allied with whom. We are able to keep the story straight, even if we miss a few words, because the composition facilitates the story. In fact, you are less likely to lose words in a well-composed show, because your attention is focused on the speaker, and you can read the body, the lips, and hear the inflection. You get the point from the composition, even if you miss the words.

Avoid These Common Composition Pitfalls

Directors, avoid some common amateur pitfalls in composition.

1. Never have your large cast stand in a straight line across the back of the stage. Aside from the fact that it looks shoddy, it blocks entrances and exits.

2. Never have your large cast stand in a semi circle around the soloist. This happens a lot in operettas, when the Major General sings "I am the very model of a modern major general," and the chorus responds, ""He thought so little, they rewarded he, by making him the ruler of the queen's Navee." (I know I'm mixing up *HMS Pinafore* with the *Pirates of Penzance*, but you get the idea.) It happens in lots of operettas. Don't do it. It looks terrible, it focuses the voices toward the wings, and it restricts the soloist to a narrow circle of movement at the center of the semi circle.

3. Don't sit your cast down in couches. There are exceptions to this, but very few. A couch is awkward to get in and out of, so, the net result is that people stay put. There is no movement. Very bad practice. There is a very funny scene in *I Love You, You're Perfect, Now Change* where the husband is watching football on tv and his wife is annoyed that he is wasting time watching football. Now, in that case, because the point is that he is wasting time on the couch, it is OK to put him on a couch. But, for the average living room scene, avoid that couch like it was made of quicksand. If you must sit on the couch, try sitting on the arm, or leaning on the back of the couch, or sprawling across the couch. Those are positions from which you can move quite easily. The one saving grace of a couch is that usually actors can also stand behind the couch, or lean over it, making for some nice composition opportunities.

4. Don't tell actors to back-up. Never ask an actor to walk forward, speak or sing the line, then walk backwards, back to the assigned position. Movement on stage should be motivated by a desire to go somewhere, to accomplish something, to communicate with someone. Backing up after a line is like a denial of motivation. This rule can be broken in opera, where there are multiple singers down front, and each may step forward one step to sing, then step back one step. The Children von Trapp in *The Sound of Music* stepped forward then back as they introduced themselves. So there are rare exceptions, but generally, don't let actors back up. They should turn and walk, motivated, to where they need to go next.

5. Don't motivate movement toward an assigned spot on the stage. Movement should be motivated, toward, or away from someone else, or toward a needed prop, such as a telephone. It should never be motivated toward or away from an assigned spot on the stage. I was watching a Broadway production recently, and in the finale an actor looked at the floor as he moved precisely to his assigned position for the final tableau. I was shocked. It pulled me completely out of the moment, and switched me into the mode of noting that they were just actors, not characters. Granted, it was a tiny faux pas, but it was indeed a reminder that even the finest performers and directors in America can make these mistakes. There are exeptions, of course, like when you are setting up for the finale in an opera, and the leads must be spaced properly across the front, but even then, encourage them to find a motivation for the move that is greater than simply getting to their assigned spot.

6. Don't let actors speak upstage. Actors in a free-blocked show will often discover themselves falling into a position of being upstaged until they get familiar with some simple solutions to that problem. It is up to the director to note it immediately, and remind them of solutions. No upstage talk. Notice this rule is not about always facing the audience, or never turning your back to the audience, as it is often taught. It is about not talking upstage. There is a difference, which you will understand more fully after the discussion of strength of body position and how to give and take.

Now, there are very positive things you CAN do with your cast, and they will be revealed in the pages to follow.

Balance the Stage

A beautiful stage picture is one that is well-balanced. A well-balanced stage looks balanced. By that I mean the mass on one side of the stage roughly balances the mass on the other side of the stage and there is use of the full depth of the stage. The stage is not static. There should be regular movement. So when you compose a well balanced stage picture it is not likely to stay that way for very long. The characters move about and fill different parts of the stage.

So, when we talk about a balanced stage we are not only talking about a balanced stage picture, but also movements that are constantly re-balancing the stage. As in the scales of justice, the mass of one object on one side should equal the mass of an object on the other side, but its OK if those scales wabble back and forth.

On the stage, our objects are people, and the stage is basically three dimensional. Rather than just two sides, such as in the scales of justice, we have two sides plus an up-stage and a down-stage, plus, we have various elevations. All of those three dimensions need to balance. So, we need a better model for the stage than the scales. Our model is gravity -- Newtonian gravity. For this discussion, we will explore balance in regards to placement of the people on the stage, and will not deal with the mass of the scenery. If the scenery is well designed it already has its own balance. But this discussion will deal only with the people.

Isaac Newton in 1687 crafted his book, *Principia Mathematica,* in which he described the force of gravity. The story goes that he was sitting under a tree when an apple fell and hit him on the head which inspired him to theorize about the force of gravity and to define it. Whether it was an apple or not, it was a significant new way of thinking about the mysterious force that pulled all objects toward earth, for Newton theorized that all objects, no matter how large or small, exert a force of attraction toward all other objects. In other words, not only was the apple falling toward the earth, but the earth was, in the tiniest way, falling toward the apple.

The force of gravity between two objects, according to Newton, was affected by two principals, (1) the mass of the objects and (2) the distance from each other. The closer they are, the stronger the pull. The more distant they are, the weaker the pull. Likewise, larger objects, such as the sun, exert more pull than smaller objects, such as planets or asteroids. In addition to forces that pull objects toward one another, there are forces of movement that tend to throw them apart. When the forces are perfectly balanced, objects remain in orbit around each other.

The most important part of Newton's theory is to realize that all bodies exert gravity upon each other. That means the moon does not revolve around a stationary earth. Rather, the earth and the moon revolve around each other. There is a center of gravity, somewhere between the earth and the moon that is the balance point and the two celestial bodies revolve around that center of gravity. Since the earth has the larger mass, the center of gravity is much closer to the earth than to the moon, so it appears from earth that the moon does all the revolving, but that is not the case. They revolve around each other, or, more specifically, they revolve around the center of gravity. The simplest, yet most effective example of the center of gravity in staging a play is the counter. When Character Jason crosses down left in front of and past Character Sara, she counters by moving somewhat to the right. Her counter is a partial revolution about the center of gravity between them.

On stage, we use those same principals to create a balance, or an orbit. The "mass" of an object could be described as the visual size of a person or group of people. Generally speaking, unless a costume makes a person oversized, we consider each single person as one unit of mass. The difference in mass, then, is usually the size of the group. A group of five people carries five times the mass of a single person.

Orient Blocking about the Center of Gravity

Imagine a spot on the center line of the stage, about one third to one half of the way upstage from the front of the apron. Define that spot as your center of gravity. Everything revolves, or, better yet, moves in seemingly random fashion about that center of gravity. Like electrons zipping randomly around a nucleus, our characters zip about that center of gravity.

Use Flat Balance in Limited Formal Situations

Flat balance is when characters are on the same plane, with equal numbers on either side of the center of gravity. Imagine two characters standing on either side of that center of gravity talking to one another. The stage is balanced. Place those same two characters anywhere on the same plane, on opposite sides of that center of gravity, equidistant from the center of gravity, no matter how far, and the stage remains balanced.

Now add two more characters, put them on opposite sides of the center of gravity, the same distance apart, and the stage remains balanced. You could add as many characters as you want, so that the mass of the groups grow, and if you put them equidistant from the center of gravity on the same plane, the stage remains balanced. Leonardo de Vinci's *The Last Supper* is an example of flat balance. Christ is in the center. There are six disciples on each side of the center. In fact, Da Vinci did better than that. He made there be two groups of three people on each side of Christ.

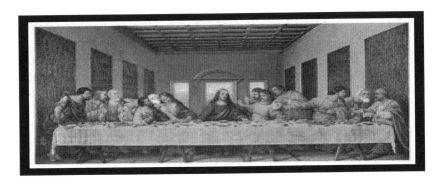

In reality, however, it is rare that you will stage all your characters on the same plane equidistant from the center of the stage unless you are staging certain scenes in *A Chorus Line*. Flat balance is static and artificial, best used in formal situations. Nevertheless, it represents a rudimentary balancing of the stage.

Use Center Balance for Large Scenes and Large Groups

More complex than flat balance, Center Balance takes into account the relative strength of body position (ranging from full front to full back) and stage position, ranging from up stage to down stage and right or left stage, and levels. A character who is in a strong body position but is far from the center of gravity can balance a person who is closer to the center but has a weaker body position. As those two characters move about the stage they should move about that center of gravity. The further away from that center, the stronger the body position one must take to retain balance. The closer to the center of the stage, the less strength of body position is required to keep the scene in balance.

Side-coach: *Balance the stage.*

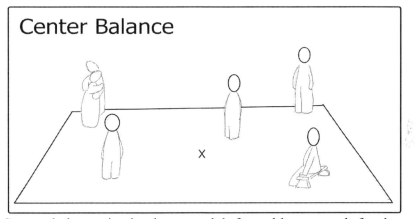

Center balance is the best model for tableaux, and for large groups on stage. For example, when there is a large mass of people singing in a chorus, and there is a soloist standing alone, the soloist must stand in a position strong enough to balance the weight of the chorus. If the entire chorus is up right, the soloist should be down left, because the downstage position is much stronger, and that strong position is needed to offset the mass of the larger chorus, and to pull the center of gravity back toward the center. If the chorus is too massive for the soloist to balance, then the chorus could be split into two, one up left and one up right. Then the soloist can work the entire down stage, including swinging from left to right, and the stage will be balanced. Or the chorus could move closer to the center, so the soloist's mass doesn't have so far to pull the chorus toward the center of gravity. The soloist would still have to work the downstage opposite side, but with more flexibility. Or, the chorus could be spread in well-spaced groups across the breadth of the upstage areas. Then the soloist could work the entire front of the stage, left, right, and center, and the stage would be balanced.

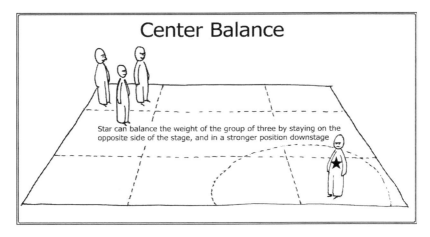

Use Off-Center Balance in Small Scenes

Small scenes do not need to balance around the center of the stage. They may take place entirely in one section of the stage, but even so, there should be a center of gravity for that area, and the scene moves about that center of gravity. Later, a subsequent scene will be played on the other side of the stage, creating swing balance. The longer the scene, the more important it is for the center of gravity to be at center stage.

Use Swing Balance to Work Both Sides of the Stage

Swing balance is pendular, and as such is very basic, and should not be overused. It's simply a cognizance that if you work one side of the stage, you must eventually swing to the other side and use that area for awhile. Then, if there is time, swing back to the middle. Swing balance keeps you using both sides of the stage. In dance and staging of musical numbers we use swing balance a lot. The figure-8 movement is a perfect form of swing balance. Marching left then marching right creates a swing balance, as does grapevine-left followed by grapevine-right. Don't get me wrong. Swing balance does not have to be a symmetrical dance movement. It can be much more random looking, and considerably more motivated by character and situation. When I see actors working only one side of the stage and I feel the balance is getting off, I may ask them to swing to the other side, meaning someone has to motivate a larger cross that uses the other side of the stage.

Side-coach: *Swing to the other side of the stage to balance the stage.*

Unite Movement with Balance: Think "Roller-Coasters"

There is a sense of excitement about the predictable yet thrilling movement of a roller coaster, as it spins, dives, lifts, and turns tight arching corners. Now imagine three intertwined roller coasters, and you have an image of how blocking among three characters might flow. There are changes of pace. There are changes of altitude, and there is a use of the entire allotted space, from left to right, and yet always around the center of gravity, returning through its point of origin, or its balance point. Roller Coaster Balance is not a distinct form of balance, rather it is a dynamic image that illustrates the interaction of stage movement with the more static image of center balance.

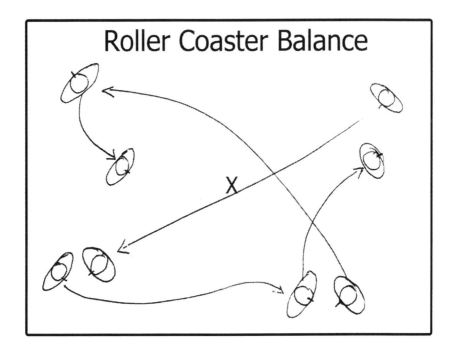

Use Circular Balance Occasionally

In circular balance actors place themselves in positions around the center of gravity. They may move about the center of gravity. The easiest form of circular balance is when you place your leading character in the center, often standing on something, and people gather around or move around that character. "Sit Down, You're Rocking the Boat" from *Guys and Dolls* might have a Gospel choir of frenzied gamblers flashing their dance hands as they circle around Nicely-Nicely. A barn dance with the caller in the center, a preacher at center with the congregation on benches around, a crowd dancing around the star in the middle, these are circular balance. Circular balance is a technique, used momentarily in choreography, or a production number, or for some symbolic moment like the ritual of burning someone at the stake. It is for occasional use only. Side-coach: *Gather in balanced clusters around the center, as though you are planets around the star;* or, *Move around the person in the center.*

Don't allow an unbalanced stage

There are a couple of don'ts that, when avoided, will help balance the stage.

1. Don't play an entire scene on one side of the stage. (Unless you play the next scene on the other side of the stage-- two scenes in a row on the same side of the stage will have the audience twisting or leaning in their seats, pulling for balance)

2. Don't put a large group on one side of the stage and leave it there (Unless you balance it with another group or a strongly placed individual).

3. Don't block people in a straight line. Straight lines are reserved for formal situations, such as a military formation, a ritual, a choir. Straight lines create an air of formality, so if your setting is at the royal palace or a state visit to the white house, by all means, put your staff in straight lines. Other exceptions include times when a line is specified by the story, such as a police line up, a queue, or a chorus line. But generally speaking, avoid straight lines as they create problems with focus and movement.

Here are some examples of various types of Balance

In a famous scene from *The Music Man*, Professor Harold Hill convinces the citizens of River City that the presence of a new pool table is serious "Trouble." He begins by speaking to one character, and then other folks notice and begin to listen, and finally a large group of citizens are whipped into hysterical fear that corruption in all its forms is about to ruin their children.

In a staging I did of *The Music Man* with a community theater I used three means of balance to stage "Trouble." Lets break that scene down into three sections:

Section 1, Center Balanced: Harold speaks only to Mr. Dunlop, the shop keeper. That scene is balanced around a center of gravity, or Center Balanced. Mr. Dunlop and Harold Hill pass on the street, passing each other near center stage. Hill calls to him, and Dunlop stops and turns to listen. Then Hill moves about the stupefied Dunlop telling him, "Ya got trouble, my friends, right here in River City." As Hill moves about, and as Dunlop watches, the scene randomly balances around that center of gravity. It is not necessary that the center of gravity be at center stage for a small scene, like the one above, as it could be played off-center. The entire scene could take place stage left or stage right. In that case, they move about a center of gravity that they establish. The longer the scene, the more important it is for the center of gravity to move to center stage. It is not as complex as the gravity analogy makes it appear. There is nothing mathematical about it. Just remember, that scenes should use the whole stage, or, if restricted by circumstance to a certain area of the stage, they should use that area fully, and then a subsequent scene should swing to the other side of the stage to balance.

Section 2. Roller Coaster Balance: As the scene progresses, more citizens join the listening audience to Professor Hill's warning. They gather in family groups that are coached to inhabit a unique space on the stage. In other words, the groups appear randomly spaced, but filling the entire stage, with open walking areas between the family groups. Then, in roller coaster balance, Harold Hill moves, or sometimes dances, in an apparently random, weaving fashion among and between the groups as he sings about the dangers of pool playing to children and as the families listen. He uses both sides of the stage, and up stage and down stage in roughly equivalent amounts. That's roller coaster balance.

Section 3. Circular Balance: In the final 3rd of the song Hill leaps to a soap box in the center of the stage and the children of River City huddle around him as though pulled by his gravity. The adults of River City repeat his refrain, "Oh We Got Trouble!" as they dance in a circle around him, like an asteroid belt orbiting around the sun.

Use Triangles:

Triangles are the simplest and most common way to create balance. A conversation between three people is in a triangle. Triangles work when there are three people on stage, but they also work for three groupings, or three objects, or any combination of people and groups. Lets start with three people. Any time there are three people on stage, unless they are in a straight line, there is a triangle, and the apex of that triangle is generally the stronger position. Other actors can take a stronger position if the person at the apex weakens, but, generally, the apex is a strong position. For that reason, when our hero is trying to convince his henchmen to agree to his plan, he is at the apex of the triangle, and pulls them toward him, with his arms around their shoulders. Or, when the police detective bursts into the room after overhearing a plot to kill someone, the detective should enter near up center and if the two conspirators separate it leaves the detective at the apex of the triangle.

Triangles are a form of center balance. **If the center of gravity is within that triangle it will be balanced.** If the center of gravity is outside the triangle that is OK, but in order to balance, there will need to be some swing balancing at a later point. In other words, the positioning will need to shift to the other side of the stage at some later point. If you begin with one triangle, the movement of any one character to another part of the stage still results in a triangle. The beauty of a triangle is that it helps create focus on the person who is at the apex. Four people on stage can also form a triangle, if two of them are clustered as one, or if one of them is weakened significantly by body position or stage position, as in the case where there is a patient dying in bed (weak position) and there are three other people in the room.

Ask for Triangles in the Set

The director and scene designers should work to assure that there are triangles in the set, A simple placement of three go-to objects in the three corners of the set will help motivate actors to work toward the triangles. Go-to objects are things like a telephone, a window, a lamp post to lean against, and a bar. It is easier to create motivated and natural movements in an interior set if one has a go-to object in each corner. People go to the bar for a drink, people go to the window to look for the missing person, and people go to the phone to call for help. These objects, positioned at the corners, create a natural triangle.

Last week I saw the Broadway production of *In The Heights*. The set was a street corner in Washington Heights, and it was constructed in triangles. There was a triangle of main entrances from the streets: Down Left, Down Right, and Up Right of Center. There was a triangle of store fronts: a taxi dispatcher down right, a convenience store up center, and a hair salon down left. Other go-to objects were a stoop beside the taxi dispatch, and a rolling cart selling shaved ice, and a street lamp or two as well as a clever way of rolling the interior of each set out into the open central stage whenever they wanted to enlarge the acting space of that particular location. The scene designer understood the value of triangles in the set and go-to set pieces.

Remind Individuals to Balance the Stage

The complex stage has characters in various places at various times. There is movement between groups, and there are tableaux being formed at different times at different places. There are crosses and counters; there are open spaces and tight groups. There are large masses and single individuals. A balanced stage uses the full complement of space, not just down center. But it does not fill all of the space with people. Empty space is very important to creating a visually strong composition too. No matter how many people are on the stage, there must be open spaces among them, among the clusters of people. More on that later, when we discuss how to create effective groupings.

A single individual can balance a larger mass by increasing the distance from that mass and by bringing the individual downstage to a stronger position. Conversely, a single individual who stands near a large mass will be absorbed into that mass, as if gravity is pulling them together. When there is a large group and a single individual on stage, think of the individual as a random comet, zipping about, being yanked by the large mass. In order to keep from being dragged by the gravity of the black hole the individual moves past the mass quickly, and can stop on the far side. Zip by and relax in outer space, then get pulled in again and zip past in the other direction, and then relax in outer space. That gravitational image may help in both movement and presenting a balanced stage.

With all this in mind about balanced composition, the next task is to teach, or encourage actors to create these balanced stage pictures as an extension of their character and the demands of the story. But don't worry. They do not have to know how to balance the stage. That is your job. What they need to know is how to follow your side coaching about staging themselves.

In order for the director to balance the stage composition in a collaborative fashion, the director must teach the actors about balance, and teach them to respond to side-coaching about balance. The director should teach the following strategies that include building the skills of balancing the stage:
    (1) take your own space, (open spacing)
    (2) form tight groups, (clusters)
    (3) counter
    (4) motivate crosses that use the entire stage
    (5) respond to each other's crosses with an eye for balance
    (6) flow from tableau to tableau, and
    (7) manifest relationships.

It is up to the director to teach and side coach them in the above and to assure that each actor is involved in solving the stage picture challenges. For example, if only one character is doing all the crosses, we have gained little. Everyone needs to commit to the movements, and it is up to the director to encourage that. Groupings, as I will discuss later, have multiple dimensions and it is easy for novices to lose track of those dimensions, so the director must side coach those as well.

Study Visual Composition in Works of Art

For the visual composition on the stage the director is the painter, or, more appropriately, the sculptor; the sculptor of moving statues. The playwright is the dramatic composer and the director follows the dramatic composer, but the director is responsible for sculpting with human bodies, for bringing the playwright's words to the stage with visual impact. Traditionally the director sculpts the actors' movements and positions with an iron hand and a velvet tongue. But in a free-blocked show, the director challenges the actors to discover movements in response to their character, the subtext they read from others, and their skill at selecting meaningful movements and beautiful body positions.

Here are some thoughts about visual composition. This is not to be considered a complete treatise on visual composition. The dedicated stage director will study other art forms that include visual composition, including photography, painting, drawing, dance, film, and sculpture. The dedicated director will also study the works and writings of other theater and film directors, gathering their ideas into a living compendium of inspiring concepts.

First, learn to look at the works of other, highly accomplished directors, through the lens of composition. Look at still photos from well-staged play performances. Take inspiration from the directors who have gone before you. In all cases, the photos they have selected for publication are well-staged moments, usually of tableaux. Notice the use of levels in both the set and the positioning of the actors. Note the use of symmetry and asymmetry. Notice how light is used to create or reinforce dramatic effect. Notice how your eyes are drawn to certain centers of focus by lines, mass, color, eye focus, and light intensity. Notice how the stage is balanced. Notice how there is a visual unity, with costume, or style, or color, or positioning. Notice how the actors' positioning tells a dramatic story. Notice how it is clear who is aligned with whom. Notice the emotional elements. Notice how often the scenery is symbolic, or suggestive, or stylized, or minimalist, rather than realistic, and notice how such scenery gives emotional force to the positioning of the actors. Notice how the set provides a variety of levels for actors to stand or sit upon. Notice the suspended gestures: poses that could be held for dramatic effect. Notice how costumes are often designed to flow or drape, reinforcing the grace of various poses.

Look too at great paintings. Look especially at great paintings of groups of people, for it is in those groupings that the stage director will find inspiration. Google these images and look at these powerful paintings and notice not only the composition, but also the picturization, which is the business of handling props, emoting, and relating to others that tells the story. Consider Leonardo Da Vinci's The Last Supper; Winslow Homer, Boys in a Pasture and Prisoners at the Front; Rembrandt's The Night Watch; Theodore Gericault, The Raft of the Medusa; George Seurat, Sunday on the Grande Jatte; Michaelangelo's Holy Family; Norman Rockwell, People in a Theater Balcony, Homecoming Marine, Freedom of Speech, Breaking Home Ties; Winslow Homer, Children on the Beach, Prisoners at the Front, Boys in a Pasture, Dressing for the Carnival; Picasso, Saltimbanques; and Pierre Auguste Renoir, Luncheon of the Boating Party, The Artist Family.

Create Visual Variety and Unity Simultaneously

Visually, it is important to create variety and unity simultaneously. Change the elements of the stage picture, and you have variety. Keep the elements similar, and you obtain unity. Your goal is to create variety and unity simultaneously. You have an advantage over some other art forms, because the play is itself a unifying element. The same characters inhabit the entire play, providing unity. Change their costumes and you have visual variety. Keep them in the same costumes, but change their groupings, and you have introduced variety. To create variety and unity, change some elements while keeping other elements the same.

Create Variety in Stage Groupings

Provide variety in your stage groupings. Small groups, large groups, orderly groups, asymmetrical groups, groups downstage, groups upstage, groups to the left, and groups to the right. Use circles, V's, blocks, lines, and open spaces. Bring groups back to similar groupings when a plot element is repeated. Many plays are bookended with a scene at the end that reflects a scene from the beginning. Stage that ending scene with similar groupings and spacings as in the original scene.

Control the Visual Focus

Strong composition will control the visual focus. That means the audience will see what the director wants them to see. the audience will see who is speaking, they will see movements, no matter how subtle that reveal subtext and that push the plot. The audience will see actions that are essential to the plot, such as the discovery of a clue, the dropping of a clue, and the passing of incriminating evidence from one person to another.   The audience's focus will not be distracted to other areas of the stage when those important plot points are happening.   You control the focus by manipulating these elements.

By body position – the actor who is most "full front" will have the focus.

By stage area – actors in central areas have stronger focus than actors in peripheral areas.

By level – the actor on the highest level pulls focus.

By plane – the further downstage, hence closer to the audience, the stronger the pull of focus.

By triangulation – the actor at the apex of a triangle has stronger pull.

By contrast – the actor who is apart from group (i.e. sitting, while rest of cast is standing) pulls focus.

By movement – moving actor will have more focus.

Chapter 3

The Development of Free Blocking: *a rehearsal strategy*

What is free blocking, and how does it contrast to traditional blocking? Free blocking is a rehearsal strategy that coaches the actors to stage themselves in response to their character's needs in the moment. It yields an exciting quality to productions, makes the rehearsals more fun, and relieves the stress on the director.

Free blocking is the centerpiece of this book. Free blocking is a set of rehearsal strategies I have developed over a long period of time. Free Blocking is wonderfully creative, and yields awesome results for me. I am excited about sharing these strategies with you, hopefully passing along this accumulated knowledge to another generation of directors.

You would not be reading this book if you did not already know what we mean by blocking. But in order to contrast free blocking to traditional blocking, lets take a moment to review traditional blocking.

What is Traditional *Blocking*?

Here is the definition of blocking, direct from wikipedia.com, the free encyclopedia.

> *"Blocking* is a theatre term which refers to the precise movement and positioning of actors on a stage in order to facilitate the performance of a play, ballet, or opera.
>
> "The director usually determines blocking during rehearsal, telling actors where they should move for the proper dramatic effect and to ensure sight lines for the audience.
>
> "Each scene in a play is usually 'blocked' as a unit, after which the director will move onto the next scene. The positioning of actors on stage in one scene will usually affect the possibilities for subsequent positioning unless the stage is cleared between scenes. Once all the blocking is completed a play is said to be 'fully blocked' and then the process of 'polishing' or refinement begins. During the blocking rehearsal usually the assistant director or the stage manager (or both) take notes about where actors are positioned and their movement patterns on stage.
>
> "It is especially important for the stage manager to note the actors' positions, as a director is not

usually present for each performance of a play and it becomes the stage manager's job to ensure that actors follow the assigned blocking from night to night.

"<u>Stage blocking</u> is one of the most basic and technical elements of play direction, but should never be taken lightly by the director. Indeed there are a few other elements of a play that are more exciting and glamorous, but blocking provides the backbone and structure needed to make those other elements a reality. Basically, blocking is the choreography of actors' movements throughout the entire play. If a character needs to exit the scene, for example, the actor must be able to move naturally towards the exit. The director's goal is to come up with a plausible means of getting that actor across the stage and through the door, window, transporter beam or whatever. The same holds true for a character delivering a monologue- should they break away from the other actors or deliver the speech in the middle of a crowd? Other considerations when blocking may include entrances of a character, or places for actors to go when their character has no function in the scene."

Notice terms like, "precise movement and positioning" and "the director determines blocking" and "telling actors where they should move." Blocking, in its traditional sense creates fixed positions and prescribed movements for actors during the earliest rehearsals, and represents considerable work for the director, making choices, planning, controlling, and being solely responsible for the visual impact of the show.

What is *Free Blocking*?

Free Blocking is a Rehearsal Technique

In contrast to traditionally blocked shows, in free blocking the actors, not the director, determine much of the blocking. The movements and positioning flex throughout much of the rehearsal process. The cementing of precise, repeated positioning and movement of actors occurs late, rather than early, in the rehearsal process.

The blocking decisions are based two concepts, (a) the **principles of stage composition** and (b) the **physicalization of emotions.**

Free blocking is a directed rehearsal technique that teaches actors the principles of staging and then encourages them to develop stage movement collaboratively in response to the needs of their characters.

In free blocking, rather than starting with blocking at the first rehearsal after the read through, we start with teaching the principles of stage composition, then we move into a period of experimentation and discovery, and as the rehearsals progress the blocking eventually firms itself. A free blocked show is firmly blocked before show time, but is flexible enough to handle any emergency or surprise on stage during a show.

Do not confuse a free-blocked show with an un-blocked, poorly blocked, or loosely blocked show. They are polar opposites. Free blocking is a method of achieving a highly effective stage composition. It is a rehearsal technique. By show time the free blocked show is tight, firmly blocked, predictable, and well paced. A free blocked show should look exactly the same at each performance. An audience member should not be able to tell the difference visually between a free-blocked show and a very well-sculpted pre-blocked show, except perhaps that it is more effective at revealing the rich undercurrents of the story.

Free Blocking is Collaborative

A free blocked show arrives at show readiness through a collaborative process among the actors, a process that gives them great awareness of the entire stage picture and the ability to adjust the stage picture on the fly. Actors help each other learn. They learn to respond to each other in character. They provide leadership to one another. They discuss the themes in open and helpful forums. In some cases, they lead or participate in rehearsal teams. They do these things through activities led by the director, as outlined in this book.

Free Blocked Actors are Not Stressed by "Catastrophes"

For amateur companies the adaptability that comes with free blocking can be a tremendously valuable skill. If your show goes on the road, playing various venues, you know how the venues can change. Some stages are larger or smaller. Some have a thrust. Some are shallow. Some are deep. Sometimes the performance space doesn't have the backstage crossover you are used to. Or that crossover is outdoors and a heavy snow or rain is falling. Sometimes you are not on a stage at all, but are in a library, or a park, or a conference room. You get the idea. The best blocking in the world can be distorted by changes in the stage space. It can be terribly frustrating for actors who have been traditionally blocked who are used to making an entrance from a certain spot and that spot is now obstructed. They all want to know where to make their entrance, or exit, and everyone on the stage needs to have new blocking to accommodate the changes. The anxiety level rises quickly, and they all look for the director to tell them, and to rehearse them, and to calm their nerves.

In contrast, in a free-blocked show, the actors are so adept at composing on the fly that they are quite facile at making adjustments. Other factors sometimes force adjustments on the fly. Factors such as an actor who can't be at the show that night because of a death in the family or a car accident in the snow on the way to the show, or a student who is suddenly ineligible for falling grades or for getting caught smoking. These things happen in school and community theater, and the show must go on. Actors must adapt to changes. Actors in free-blocked shows hardly blink an eye. Even actors with no prior experience in free blocking will have such confidence by show time that they could accommodate just about any problem they encounter.

If you've directed many shows, you know that catastrophes happen. A chair collapses, a wig falls off, the jar of pickles won't open, the tea tray breaks a leg, an important prop can't be found, the gunshot sound effect doesn't happen, the lamp that is supposed to be on the desk that rolls on isn't there, the ingenue's dress rips open in the back as she walks on stage, an actor misses an entrance, an actor skips several lines or forgets the lines altogether, a set piece gets left on by mistake during a scene change. You know. These things happen. In a traditionally blocked show actors don't dare leave their blocked spot to go fix the problem, or, if they do, they do awkward things to get back to their original assigned spot. So the problem hangs over the scene like a giant elephant in the room that no one dares acknowledge or fix. But in a free blocked show, actors feel completely comfortable about moving around to fix a problem, and others adjust, and it's just no big deal.

A True Story about A Catastrophe Avoided.

In one show I directed using free blocking there was an important role played by a child. In a climactic moment of the play the child got confused and made a dramatic running entrance from the wrong side of the stage. The direction of his entry was important to the rest of the staging. This was a free-blocked show and I watched in amazed and satisfied wonder as the entire small ensemble instantly reversed the blocking into a mirror image of the original. Everyone adjusted as though they had always rehearsed it this way. The scene worked perfectly. When I congratulated everyone for their quick thinking in our de-briefing, their response was nonchalant. It was no big deal to them. If, on the other hand, it had been a traditionally blocked show, it would have been a very different response. There would have been considerable stress, blaming, and shaming going on, combined with under-the-breath comments about never again doing a show with children. I've seen it both ways. Believe me, I prefer the free-blocked method.

True story. Stress reduction is a good thing in the theater.

Free Blocking is Effective with All Skill Levels

Free blocking is effective with all skill levels of actors. This director has worked with children, high schools, community theater, college theater, and, once-upon-a-long-time-ago, in professional theater. Free-blocking works with large groups, small ensembles, opera, musicals, and straight plays. It works on a proscenium, in the round, in a converted barn, or any variation. It only works, however, if the director has a very strong understanding of quality composition and stage movement, and if the director is comfortable with facilitating rather than dictating.

The director will understand how movement affects focus, how movement reveals subtext, how humor is released, and how to teach staging skills to actors in a relatively short amount of time. And the director will teach these things to the actors both in small workshops before the rehearsals begin in earnest, and in little mini-workshops along the way. Above all, the director will enjoy inviting the creative genius in each actor to flourish while still maintaining artistic control of the finished product. That balancing act will be your greatest interpersonal accomplishment.

I used free blocking in a children's Christmas play for a community theater. and I found that eighth graders, with little previous theater experience, latched onto the concepts quickly. It was only a few rehearsals into the schedule when I saw actors making sophisticated movements, balancing the stage, and motivating approach and avoidance moves in response to the struggles their character was feeling. I was impressed. The only thing that bothered me was the realization that they would probably do their next show with a traditional blocking director, and they would feel frustrated by the limits placed on them by that method. I had given them acting skills they would have to stifle in the future. Well, maybe not, if enough directors read this book.

Free Blocking Can be Taught and Learned Quickly

In the following pages we will provide you with the tools you need to be a genius at free-blocking.

You will learn to give quick interactive workshops, maybe 15 minutes in length, that teach actors what they need to know. You will learn how to sidecoach them during rehearsals, coaching them to remember to use the strategies they learned in those workshops. You will learn quick ways to review those workshops with exercises that take as little as 15 seconds, so that each rehearsal can begin with warmups that review the free blocking strategies.

It will be up to you to implement them in a comprehensive fashion. Don't skip steps. Don't give up the artistic leadership. Don't look at free blocking as a way to drift through the rehearsal process. Rehearsals will demand your attention but in a new way. Rather than trying to always have the right answer to tough question, you will become adept at asking open-ended questions that actors can easily answer. Rather than telling actors what to do you will become adept at asking them what their character feels like doing and what internal struggle prevents them from doing it and what movement could express that struggle. Rather than showing them what to do to be funny, you will learn to help them discover the props and movements that express genuinely funny human foibles. And throughout all of this you will keep them practicing and refining their skills at balancing the stage, creating attractive groupings, and revealing the constant changing of relationships and focus through the conventions of stage movements and body positions.

You have your work cut out for you. But it should be immensely rewarding, and considerably less stressful than the old way. In the old way, the pressure was on you to be the decider, the inventor, the creative genius, the answer-giver, and the best actor. In the free blocked show, you will be the facilitator, the inspiration, the coach, and the one who helps everyone feel connected to the show.

Don't get me wrong. Leaders in the theater must be super-prepared and in control. I want my musical director to insist upon notes, rhythms, entrances, cut-offs, and phrasing that are precise and fantastic. I want my choreographer to come to each dance rehearsal with the steps worked out in advance, and with a time-efficient rehearsal routine for teaching, practicing, and refining the movements. I want our technical directors to arrive at load in and tech with their sets, costumes, lights, and sound in top condition, and with their crew well trained, and their cues prepared.

The director, too, must have a well-thought through rehearsal schedule, production meetings, and leadership to use the time of all personnel efficiently. There is a time for decisiveness, rigor, standards, and accountability. It is up to the director and his appointed agents to insist upon high standards. Never confuse the free blocking rehearsal strategy with a laissez-faire attitude toward quality and accountability. No. Free blocking achieves the highest level of staging. You want all of the other production values to be commensurate. Insist upon it, model it, encourage it, and reward it.

How did I get here?

I didn't start my career in directing using free blocking. I was trained in directing in my undergraduate years in some very traditional methods. I found that all the books on directing, and all the effective directors with whom I worked were using similar strategies, at least in a fundamental way. They approached the composition in a traditional fashion, by writing blocking into the stage manager's book, and locking it in during early rehearsals. Some of them were wonderfully inspiring. Some were good acting coaches. Most of them had some great qualities that made them be admired and followed. Generally they got good reviews from the press, from their actors, from their production teams, and from their audiences. I liked what I saw and I wanted to be a director, too. Though I had directed a couple shows while I was still in high school, I really caught the bug in my sophomore year of college, and began to look for as many opportunities to direct as possible, and to hone my skills, sell myself as a potential director, and build my repertoire of plays. By the time I graduated from the University of Southern Maine with a major in theater I had directed a healthy handful of shows, scenes, musical events, and performance events at college, the local high school, a new professional summer theater, and a USO tour. The year after graduation I founded my first children's theater and began teaching and directing in a high school. Next came community theater, another children's summer theater, community opera, more high schools, and, by the age of 30 I had directed over 100 shows, and the number was still climbing. I lost count shortly after that, as I was busy directing with my local high school, directing in my third children's theater, and in two community groups. Over the years I've done the mime thing, the clown-juggler thing, the story-teller thing, the puppeteer thing, singer-songwriter thing, and the playwright thing. I've done set designs, scene painting, construction, lighting, and make-up for shows in the area. I've never done costumes, as there has always been someone around who is much better than I at that. I've been a husband to a beautiful wife and a father to five boys, all of whom are theater buffs and occasional performers. Two of them have performed professionally, and one has had a pretty good stint on Broadway. I am now over 60 years old, a retired high school principal. I have a couple more degrees, and all but the dissertation for a doctorate in educational leadership. I quit the doctoral thing because I needed more time to be an artist, and less time devoted to being a researcher. I am still directing plays whenever I get a chance.

The development of the Free Blocking rehearsal strategy took years to emerge from my experiences into something that is ready to be passed along to the next generation of directors. Following are three fundamental discoveries that emerged from the frustrations of directing community and school theater that helped shape my strategy. First is the emerging realization that actors can be creative geniuses; second is the problem of staging large groups in attractive arrangements on stage when there is always one or more actors absent from rehearsal; and the third is the problem that blocking stagnates or restricts movement, when movement is the vehicle for revealing subtext, for capturing the audience's eye, and for cracking up the audience with humor. Here are some examples to illustrate those discoveries.

I Learned That Some Actors are Creative Geniuses

In the middle of my career as a director, sometime after that 100th show, and after years of using traditional pre-blocking and early blocking rehearsals to shape the actors' positions and movements on stage I stumbled upon the concept that some of my actors are creative thinkers. I was not looking for that creativity. In fact I was rather possessive about my staging, feeling that I could create flowing crosses and counters, well balanced composition, and a stage picture that was beautiful and effective at telling the story, without interference from the actors. Their job was to act within the blocking. My job was to work the big picture, the part they could not see, and to shape them, as an artist would compose the elements of a painting, such that there was a beauty and balance to the composition.

I know that sounds arrogant, but, (gulp!) I was arrogant and just couldn't see it. Of course I listened to the actors, helped them find motivation for the crosses, and adjusted blocking to accommodate their needs, but basically, I was in charge of the stage picture.

Little things began to change my image of how a show ought to be approached. Lots of little things actually. Books I read, counseling courses I took, teaching strategies I was using in my classroom, feedback from my actors and my audiences, and teachable-learnable moments in life. There were many, but, to illustrate here is one incident that helped me rethink.

True Story About an Actor's Idea that Was Much Better Than Mine.

It was during dress rehearsal of *Princess Ida*, an opera by Gilbert and Sullivan, and one of the first nights we were rehearsing with the full set. An actor came to me with a suggestion that used the set in a way we had not thought of during rehearsal. The creative genius was Steve, our local super-tenor. To appreciate his idea, let me describe the scene. *Princess Ida* is set in a protected and isolated medieval women's college, no men allowed, with scenery of great stone towers, ivy covered walls, and a giant gate. The humor comes when a trio of guys decide to scale the walls and enter the women's private domain, to enjoy viewing the girls. And for Hilarion (played by Steve) the goal was to finally see the princess he has been betrothed to since birth.

To avoid detection the boys throw on some ill-fitting female academic robes, and sneak about flirting with one beautiful girl after another, until they finally get caught and are thrown in the off-stage dungeon. But Steve looked at the great stone tower of the set with a window in it and suggested his prison be not a dungeon, but rather in the tower. I resisted at first, this being dress rehearsal. But, I relented and we tried it. His dungeon was now <u>onstage</u> rather than offstage. And from that window he longed for every sight of his betrothed princess. He sighed as she soliloquized in song and savored her beauty as she passed by below him, oblivious of his admiration. It was cute, as though right out of a fairy tale, and it was effective, revealing considerable subtext, and some dramatic irony, and I had not thought of doing it. Furthermore, I had never asked the actors if they had any ideas that could enrich the show. So it took a guy with enough chutzpah to challenge me to bring his creative idea into the play. I liked it. We kept it. And I decided at that moment that I would be better off soliciting creative ideas from the actors during the rehearsal process, so that all the collective creative genius of our team could be engaged in enriching our shows. It was not a watershed moment, but it was at least a good illustration of the influences that shaped my desire to develop a more inclusive rehearsal process.

True story. Actors are creative geniuses. We directors need to plan how to access that genius rather than stifling it.

"I like it. Keep it!" became a new catch phrase for creative ideas, an affirmation to the actor that the creative impulse yielded an effective movement.

Steve's choice was not free blocking, so don't misunderstand. In fact it was a risk, to try something that had not been worked out in rehearsal. What it was, however, was an expression by an actor of a creative idea risk, and it worked. To prevent such things from happening at dress rehearsal, or later, it is important that we as directors access the actors' creativity during rehearsal.

Incidents like that led me to invent and borrow from other directors and thinkers. My learning curve about directing once again went up a steep hill. I wanted to know who had creative ideas, and I began to develop strategies that encouraged more creative input from the actors, and to do it in a way that was consistent with the artistic whole. Some of my strategies were less effective, but eventually I found myself approaching the rehearsal with more of an open book, with pages still blank.

I also noticed that some actors became more engaged in generating ideas, but that it was frustrating when those new ideas had to be tried in an environment where the blocking was already set. A small change in blocking would create a ripple effect in the blocking. We kept having to change whole scenes of blocking well into the rehearsal process to accommodate creative ideas, new discoveries in relationships, comic business, and movements that revealed subtext. Something had to give because actors got frustrated with constant changes in the blocking.

Add to that the limited rehearsal time of amateur theater, and then complicate that with the absentees at some rehearsals, and the difficulty of keeping the stage managers blocking book up-to-date, and the result was that changes in the blocking one day became problematic for several subsequent rehearsals. Something had to be done differently. This whole directing thing was too stressful.

I Learned that Absenteeism Screws up Blocking

The second great lesson in the development of *free blocking* was again associated with a community opera. I had the responsibility to stage large groups of people for the grand choral numbers and finales. I always enjoyed the challenge of staging large groups, for I would place them in levels, in groups and tableaux, in balanced composition, and then I would sit back in the house and enjoy the visual impact of my creation. That is, until John was excused from rehearsal for his daughter's wedding, and Sara was home sick, so their groups had holes in them, and Bill, Joanie, and Kayla, who missed the original blocking rehearsal, showed up, ready to be put on stage, and needed to be placed somewhere. Ouch. This was stressful.

Community theater is famous for large group scenes with people missing rehearsals. The net result is that the beautiful blocking kept changing, the groups looked sloppy, and the new people had no way to integrate themselves without the director telling them where to go. Come show time, and it was dress rehearsal before we had everyone on stage for the large group scene, and all my great composition was now a mess due to overcrowding and confusion about who was supposed to be where Absenteeism had made a mess of my great composition. I wasted a lot of time at subsequent rehearsals solving the problems associated with absenteeism. I wasted a lot of emotional energy. Anger was becoming too frequent for me, and it was interfering with my own enjoyment of the art of directing. I needed a better way.

I Learned that Actors can Form Their Own Tight Groups

Out of this experience came the grouping rehearsals, a fundamental concept of free blocking. I taught people how to create their own well-shaped groups, and how to adjust when a person was added or removed from the group. I taught them to use levels, spacing, touch, asymmetry, and a variety of parameters to create professional looking tableaux in seconds. I have refined those training strategies over the years such that in a 45 minute interactive workshop I can teach a cast of amateurs to create tableaux on cue. Those strategies are outlined in this book.

Do the groups work? Yes. There is an International Cup winner to support it. In 1994 the Gilbert and Sullivan Society of Hancock County USA won the International Trophy at the Gilbert and Sullivan Festival in Buxton, England, with a production of *Utopia, Ltd.*, under the direction of Dede Johnson. Johnson used the grouping strategies of free blocking to stage the many large group numbers. The adjudicator made special notice of the effective tableaux. Furthermore, as a high school director my entries in the local, regional, state, and New England drama festivals were consistently well regarded, with many school trophies and student awards, including ensemble awards, to confirm the effectiveness of these strategies.

I Learned that Movement Keeps the Show Alive

Movement sustains interest. Movement is essential to the graceful flow of a show. Movement reveals and releases subtext, the truly engaging element of drama. Movement drives the tension and pacing. Movement is the vehicle for humor.

Let me take you back to my high school days, and perhaps your high school days as well. Winola Cooper was my high school chorus teacher and the organizer of the annual variety show. Winola was an impressive presence, with deep eyes, circled in dark shadows, and a voice that ranged from bass to soprano. I cut my teeth in show business as part of her student committee to produce the annual show. Winola believed in movement. "Get them moving!" she would bellow to her choreographer and friend, Mary Ann, of Mary Ann's School of Dance. Mary Ann would bring her corps of dancers, but she would also teach everyone to move to the music, which was usually show tunes. "Get them moving!" Winola would call out, and Mary Ann would run up on the stage and teach us all some simple steps to enliven the musical number. One memory I had from that was how much I enjoyed being part of the movement. So did the others. Kids would fight for the right to be part of the select group for each number that got to dance. Movement is much more interesting than sitting still, both as a performer and as an audience member. Audiences are drawn to movement. They quickly grow bored and their minds wander when there is no movement.

Over the years I have had the opportunity to see literally hundreds of high school one-act plays, because I was either coaching a play at a festival of 10-12 plays, Or I was serving as an adjudicator at such a festival, or, near the end of my career, I was the high school principal hosting the one-act play festival. I've seen hundreds of one-acts, some very good, especially at the level of the state finals and the New England Theater Festival, and some rather amateurish. I can tell you that plays without movement are like watching a chess match if you have never played chess. You can only watch it for so long before you need to look at something else. I have seen plays where the characters sit down on a couch and don't move until the script says they exit, sometimes 10 minutes of sitting. Ouch. My butt begins to ache. I look at the lekos and fresnels; I whisper to my wife; I read the program, hunting for something to stimulate my mind. "Get the moving!" I can hear Winola's spirit calling from her grave.

A True Story about a Bad Decision I Made.

I remember directing a community theater play, very early in my career, when two of the actors were considerably older than me, and, judging by how they talked, they projected the image that they were considerably more knowledgeable about theater. They insisted that they direct themselves in one scene, since they had such a deep understanding of the play and had some ideas they wanted to express. Foolishly, I let them do it. What a mistake! They may have had an intellectual understanding of the scene, but their movement was non existent. Though to this day I don't remember the name of the play nor the actors, I still remember the non existent blocking.

One man sat asymmetrically on the arm of a couch (his most creative decision) and the other sat nearby in a chair, and they talked. For 5 or 10 minutes, which felt like an hour, they sat there and talked. It was a comedy, and they evoked narry a chuckle. The play died, just sank like a ship with a hole in the hull. There was no emotional connection. There was no shift in relationship, although the script was loaded with discoveries, with subtext, with connivance, none of which were revealed.

The actors had discussed them intellectually between themselves, but they had no skill at translating those discussion points into movement that could be interpreted by the audience. Ultimately, and in the brink of time, I had to retake command, rehearse that scene from scratch, and deal with the attitude of the actors as best I could. I learned a huge lesson the hard way.

True story. (By the way, that was NOT an example of scene teams.)

The point is that movement does much to move a show forward. It helps actors express emotion. It draws the audience's eye. Movement changes actors' positions on stage, hence changing the relationships and the focus. Movement has tempo or pace, and can lift the scene toward a beat.

The strategies in free blocking will help get actors moving in ways to accomplish the goals of the show. When the show is properly blocked, the director subtly controls what the audience sees, from the grandest movement to the tiniest clue. Skillful blocking gives the show a gracefulness, a flow, a shaping and reshaping of beautiful stage pictures. It also engages the audience in interpreting movement. Humans are adept at deciphering body language, and audiences love to use those skills in the enjoyment of a play. Give the audience movement that expresses the subtext, and they will appreciate it much more than if they had to rely upon words and inflection alone.

Chapter 4

Advantages of Free Blocking

Free Blocking is a rehearsal strategy that frees the actors to be in the moment with their character, responding with action and movement to emerging discoveries and emotions. It allows the movements to change from one rehearsal to the next, as the actors grow into their characters, while maintaining the essentials of blocking, namely focus, relationships, and beauty.

Advantage 1. No Pre-Blocking

No pre-blocking is a huge advantage for the collaborative director, especially the director who holds a day job. Pre-blocking is a time consuming planning activity of the director. With stage diagrams, blocks of wood, model theaters, or other devices, and a very thorough understanding of each of the characters and the script, the director draws out the movements and placement of the actors, matched to specific lines in the script. In the blocking rehearsals the director mechanically places the actors on the stage, according to the pre-block plan and the actors dutifully write down their positions and movements. If the blocking is done well, it creates a strong stage picture.

In contrast, in a free-blocked show there is no pre-blocking. The director does not have to sit with diagrams, blocks of wood, or other apparatus, alone, in advance, planning out the blocking movements. No rehearsal time is wasted on writing in the blocking. Actors are not forced to justify awkward blocking with equally forced motivations for characters they have not yet fully understood. Instead, the blocking will be developed collaboratively throughout the rehearsal process.

Those early blocking rehearsals will be replaced with workshops on how to create effective stage composition in response to the movements of others, movements that are an extension of the emotions and the shifting relationships among the characters.

Advantage 2. Creative Input

Few directors (read that as no directors) can imagine, in advance, all the subtleties that actors, through their characters, can bring to the play. In fact, neither can the actors. Free blocking allows actors and directors to continually discover new subtext, to move in response to that subtext, and to do so without upsetting the blocking.

Advantage 3. Actors Develop Problem Solving Skill

Have you ever watched a mistake happen on stage, usually when a prop drops on the floor, and no one seems to dare slip out of their blocking to go fix it. Finally, the most professionally competent of the cast will gracefully pick up the prop and put it away, (good choice) and then return to his or her original position (not a good choice), but only after several moments of discomfort for cast and audience. Never would such a thing happen with a free-blocked show. In free blocking, characters are used to moving in response to new ideas, and the rest of the cast is experienced at countering, giving, and re-grouping.

I once was directing Brian Friel's play, *Translations*, in a play festival, on a stage very different in size from our home stage. During our one-hour technical rehearsal on the new stage, we quickly discovered that the stage was much deeper than our rehearsal space, and I had blocked the show much too flat. I was not using free blocking at the time, though I wish I had been. We ran to our rehearsal space and made some decisions about how to deepen our blocking, talked it over, and then went on, without a full rehearsal. The new blocking went fine until one moment when an upstage character moved from left to right to reposition herself, and at the same time, a speaking character downstage also moved from left to right. That parallel movement was horrible to behold from my seat in the audience. The judges later noted that same awkward movement. I know that if we had been using free blocking rehearsals, the upstage actor would have known to move counter, not parallel.

For example, now that I use free blocking exclusively, at a rehearsal for a small musical just last week, a 13 year old girl made a beautiful counter move when she noticed just such a downstage cross in front of her. You can't teach actors to problem solve if they never have to solve a problem until show time. You can teach them to problem solve if their entire rehearsal regimen is about reacting in character to whatever happens on stage.

Even experienced actors get incapacitated by problems on stage if they are strictly blocked. I watched a show recently where an actress's wig came off as she was doing a walkover handstand over a man's lap. Her character was practicing a show dance number where she was the floozie entertaining a group of soldiers. Her wig caught on the soldier's shirt and stayed there, all blond and curly, hanging from his chest, as she went on with the dance, after a moment of shock. The soldier-actor was flustered, couldn't un-snag the wig, and quickly ran off the closest exit. The Show girl finished the scene, and the next scene, without the wig. Nothing was said. Nothing was done. The show went on with the original blocking. But there was this giant elephant in the room that no one was acknowledging... A floozie without any flooze on her head, a missing wig, and a flustered missing soldier.

It was truly better to continue on, rather than to break, but it was very awkward for a long time. Considering that this was a comedy, and if the soldier had remained in character, it might have been well within his character to enjoy the wig caught on his chest, as well as the other soldiers around.

The dancer character would have done well to demand the wig back, and some soldiers help her get it back, and suddenly you have one of the most classic comic situations, two people wanting or needing the same object. (Called, "Give me That;" more on that later) Of course it would have screwed up all the well planned and rehearsed blocking, but it would have worked much better than the way it was handled, trying to ignore it. Set-in-stone blocking inhibits discovery, both in rehearsal and in the show. Had that been a free-blocked show, the characters would have handled the problem much more in character and within the context of the show, I'm sure.

Advantage 4. Motivation is Inherent.

Probably the most frustrating experience for an actor is when the director gives a blocking movement, accompanied by no explanation of the motivation, or at best, an inadequate one. "What's my motivation?" is a common and important question, although, in a dictatorial environment that question may never be asked. Then comes the struggle for the actor to integrate the director's explanation into their own emerging sense of the character.

As an actor myself, I find it frustrating to be told to stand somewhere on the stage when I feel motivated to move somewhere else. Or to be told to make a small movement on a particular line, and then a large movement on the next line. I find myself focusing on the movement, rather than on the emerging understanding of character. I especially dislike it when the director has misplaced me, such as placing me in center stage, when I am not the center of focus. Or, if I have to speak to another character but there is someone in my way, blocking my view of the character to whom I am speaking. Or if I am struggling to understand what is going on between two other characters, but I am blocked to be off to the side, rather than between them (See, Put the Struggler in the Middle). The director often places characters with a minimal understanding of what the blocking does to affect how characters can or cannot develop.

On the other hand, in free blocking, it is often the actor, coached by the director, who discovers the motivation to move, and who actually selects where to move and how far. Actors also move in reaction to the movements of other actors, again, as motivated by the character at the discretion of the actor. The director simply coaches, encourages, or shapes those movements. There are times, however, when the director shapes a movement as a set-up.

The easiest explanation of a set-up is to imagine that one cannot move <u>toward</u> a precious object unless one has been set up <u>away</u> from that object. Getting away is the set up for the movement toward the object. One cannot make a powerful move to down front center unless one has been set up somewhere further upstage. Getting upstage is the set up for the grand moment of taking center stage. Sometimes, too, the director wants a particular tableau for the ending, and there is some set up that precedes movement to that final tableau. Generally, though, throughout the free-blocked rehearsal process, much of the movement is developed by the actor in response to the needs of their character and the movements of other characters on stage.

Advantage 5. Comfort on Stage

Some actors need creative input. Some request the security of knowing where to go and where others are going to be. Free blocking gives both. The creative process is at the beginning of the rehearsal process, and the firm blocking is at the end of the process, before show time. Regardless, most actors appreciate knowing that they can move on stage if necessary, and that other actors will have appropriate counter moves or re-groupings.

Advantage 6. Characters are More Believable

When I go to watch a show I can tell much about the rehearsal process from the believability of the characters. All too often in high school and community theater the characters are less than believable. They are stilted, stock, and marginally comfortable, often restricted by their blocking, or lack of blocking, and by their internal inhibitions. They may be trying hard, even forcing their interpretation upon the audience. They may be laboring with an accent, or over-modulating their voice, or carrying a great deal of tension thinking about their blocking, lines, and carriage. In general, they are trapped in a body that has to behave in prescribed ways and their ability to be in the moment and honest with their emotions is restricted. It is hard to be in the moment when your character feels like running or striking out at someone but you are blocked to stand still and yell.

This internal conflict restricts actors from even discovering what the character could really be feeling. It prevents actors from behaving in ways that provide physicalization of subtext that other characters can read. It closes down the subtext cycle. When subtext disappears, the characters lose their believability, and the audience must trust their own imagination to fill in the subtext, almost as though they are reading a novel instead of watching a play. The audience suspends their disbelief in the character, and fills in the gaps.

In contrast, a free-blocked show grows throughout rehearsal as the actors move in response to emotions, in response to subtext. The characters are more believable because they act, move, and discover things in response to each other. Their blocking is a function of the emerging story, and as the story grows more rich, so do the movements and tableaux.

At the same time, actors are developing their ability to see the stage, to think about composition, and to move about and form stage pictures that provide focus and that tell the story visually and beautifully. It is not as complex or difficult as it sounds. Using the techniques in this book you can teach all of your actors to be effective at composing the stage picture in as little as three workshops and some warm-up reminders at the beginning of rehearsals, and as supported by side-coaching during rehearsal.

Advantage 7. Replacement Actors Fit in Quickly

When an actor calls in sick at noon on the day of a sold out show, the community theater rushes to find a replacement. Book-in-hand the replacement goes on with barely a walk through, and no real knowledge of the blocking. In a traditional show the regular actors are confused, frustrated, and unable to adjust to the movements, if any, of the replacement actor. In a free blocked show, the adjustments are fluid and easy for the regular actors.

Likewise the replacement actor can be given a quick training in free blocking strategies, and then is free to create motivated movements, confident that the rest of the cast can adjust.

Advantage 8. Less Stress for the Director and Cast

If there is one feature of free blocking that appeals to me more than anything else, it is that there is less stress for me as a director, and less stress for the actors. That one feature is worth it all. In fact, there is much more laughter, and sheer joy in rehearsals, simply because the kinesthetic exercises I use are fun and generate humor. Who could complain about rehearsals being fun!

Chapter 5

The Principles of Free Blocking

This chapter is the quick-and-simple version of the Free Blocking process. You will teach your actors these principles before rehearsal begins, and you will remind them with mini workshops at each rehearsal. The full discussion of each process, along with how to train the actors, is in Chapters 6, 7, and 8, which cover where, how, and why actors move.

Workshops

Free Blocking trains actors in how to make decisions about their character's movement and stage positioning This is done through a series of simple workshops given to the full cast. Each chapter includes a complete scripted workshop, covering Focus, Movement, Grouping, and Motivating Movement.

All four of those workshops could be done in a single two-hour rehearsal. Or you may break them up in a way that suits your needs, but they should all be done before rehearsal from the script begins.

I have included reviews for each of the workshops, which take only a few minutes. Do the reviews at the beginning of every rehearsal. In later rehearsals these reviews can be led by members of the cast as a warm up.

Side-Coach

The most common rehearsal strategy of the facilitative director is side-coaching. This book will be filled with side-coaching tidbits, all of which are simple phrases which serve either of two purposes, (1) to evoke or (2) to remind.

When you side-coach to be evocative you are asking questions that encourage the actor to think and feel more deeply and to experience the moment more genuinely. For example: *What are you struggling with?* and *How do you feel now?* and *What else do you feel?* These simple, evocative, side-coaching questions encourage the actor to be in the moment with the character. Notice that they are addressed not to the actor, but to the character, and should be answered by the character.

However, when you side coach to remind, it is phrased as a suggestion, and is directed to the intellect of the actor. The director reminds the actor to implement the strategies of free blocking, to implement the strategies you have been teaching them in workshops. The side-coaching reminds actors by using the same words that were used in the workshop. For example: *Give!* or *Give me tight groups in 5, 4, 3, 2, 1.* or, *Put the struggler in the middle!* or, *Reach out and touch someone,* or *Hold that tableau,* or, *Check in with your listeners.* As you will see from the activities that follow, these particular side-coach phrases ask for specific skills and actions from the actors, skills they have been learning, skills they will forget to implement without your side-coaching. In summary, side-coaching to evoke is addressed to the character, and is phrased as a question that helps the character experience the moment more genuinely, whereas side-coaching to remind is addressed to the actor and is phrased as a suggestion.

Teach Actors to Take Their Own Space

"Take Your Own Space" yields awesome results very quickly. If every director would only teach their actors to "Take Your Own Space" then most of the ugly blocking I often see in amateur companies would disappear. There would be no lines, no semicircles, and no motley crowds blocking the entrances.

This one directorial command is powerful. You may have experienced the moment when you described the finale, then get ready to stage it, and tell the actors to go up on the stage. They go up, and look like an elephant herd, waiting for you to tell them all where to go. 40 people waiting for you to tell them exactly where to stand. Don't do it. Remember, someone is absent, and someone else will be absent next rehearsal. You can create all the beautiful tableaux you want, with great groups, use of the stairs, with short people down front and tall ones in the rear, etc., and they will dutifully (if reminded, and if they have pencils) write their assigned spot in the script. However, next rehearsal will be a mess. People will be missing, and people who were absent last week will now be here, and people will forget what their scribbles in their script meant. What a mess!

If it is indeed the finale, you may need to add that you want the principals downstage, but that's about it. Just tell them, "Take your own space." and they will array themselves beautifully, filling the stage, using the platforms, and all able to see the conductor. Hey. What could be easier!

The workshop at the end of this chapter will teach actors how to take their own space, how to create balanced, full stage positioning in only three seconds.

Side-coach: *Take your own space,* or, *Give me open spacing.* **To get them to move quickly I tell them**: *Take your own space and balance the stage in 3 seconds. Go! 3, 2,, 1. Freeze.*

Open Spacing -- "Take your own space."

Sailors from *South Pacific*

Note the 1/4 position with the head turned front, the relaxed body and arms, and how the give and take puts focus on the soloist.

Create Focus

Focus is a simple concept. The director wants the audience to see who is speaking, and occasionally to see certain business, props, or reactions. **Focus is the set of staging principles that pull the audience's collective eye where the director wants them to look.** In other words, the effective director controls what the audience sees, and when they see it, and even controls how to bring their wandering eyes back to the important stage action. Basically the director shapes the actors' (1) **stage position**, (2) **body position**, and (3) **movement** to create focus. In free blocking the director teaches and coaches actors into collaboratively managing their stage position, body position, and movement in a manner that creates effective composition as well as focus.

The workshop on focus teaches them to fill the stage with open spacing through the command, "Take your own space."

Teach Actors to Create Focus

The simplest way to create focus is for the actors to look at the speaker. Whoever the actors look at, the audience will also look at. I call that **eye focus**. Simply put, the actors should generally look at whoever is speaking.

If the characters' situation doesn't allow the actors to look at whoever is speaking, then wherever they look must be weaker than the character of focus, such as looking down at their feet, crying into their hands, looking out an upstage window, or reading a note, etc. **Side-coach**: *Give him/her eye focus*, or more simply, *Eye focus!* For amateurs, and children, wandering eyes are more common than we would like, and they are a distraction to the focus the director is trying to achieve. A singer who looks at the conductor, or a child who looks at Mommy in the audience, or the bored spear carrier who looks off stage at the set crew preparing the next scene, or the debutant who looks to see if her dress is flowing properly can pull eye focus away from the central action. Side-coach them to bring that focus back to the speaker.

Focus is created when the person who should be receiving the focus is in a stronger position than anyone else on stage, so actors should give focus when they are not the center of attention, and take focus when they are. I call that *Give and Take*, and it is covered in the workshops in the following chapter.

I begin each staging rehearsal with a review of aspects of staging. The director should never be lulled into thinking that actors have learned it. They have a lot to think of. You are their director. They need you to lead them. Like rehearsing lines, and playing scales on the piano, there are certain activities that are fundamental to being on stage, and must be rehearsed so much that they become second nature.

Teach Actors to Move

Actors must move as motivated by their character, the emotions, the situation, the subtext. But my experience is that actors will not move on their own. If you tell people to act a scene without any direction they will basically stand there and talk.

Free Blocking trains actors in a wide repertoire of movement choices. They learn to share, to pivot, to face away, to cross away, to cross to, to cross in front, and to cross upstage, to name a few. Further, they learn how to balance the stage. They still won't do it much without being reminded, but that is one of the director's roles in the free blocked show. Remind actors to move.

Some of the movements require people to walk away from others, or to turn away from others, and that is the hardest thing for actors to learn. They have no trouble seeing the motivation to move toward another character, but, if that happens too much, everyone gets clustered together in a big sort of stagnant mess. Someone has to be motivated to move away. So, I spend a great deal of time teaching in workshop the concept of Approach and Avoidance. Actors learn to motivate themselves to turn away or to walk away in response to subtextual conflicts.

We also run them through the paces of various movements in response to stimuli, in an effort to help them be prepared to select movements that work in particular situations. I teach them to bring energy to the blocking by running when there is urgency, fear, thrill, or a need to escape a thought or a situation. That skill includes the ability to self-motivate a stop, so that the run remains contained to the space on stage.

Rehearsals

Once you have taught the four workshops, the daily rehearsals are the easy part.

I can teach all four workshops in one two-hour rehearsal. You might take longer to start. The workshops are at the end of their appropriate chapter, chapters 6-9.

1. Review the workshops as a warmup.

2. Start at the top of the script and work through as far as you can get comfortably. Pick up where you left off next time. (Reviewing scenes over and over is optional. There is no need to repeat scenes to cement the blocking, That will come later.)

3. Your job is to SIDECOACH.

4. Your job is to hold the play true to the intention of the playwright, as best you can figure it out. The playwright can't be at the rehearsal with you, so it's up to you.

5. Your job is to be the eyes and ears of the audience. Can you see the right thing, can you hear the words, can you feel the tension? Is something not working right? Encourage the actors fix it themselves.

6. Your job is to help the actors expand themselves, as their acting coach. (Get my other

book, *Stress Free Coaching of Pre-Broadway Actors: For the Stage Director Who Has a Day Job)*

7. Assign *scene teams*, eventually, but it's best to wait until everyone is comfortable with the free blocking style.

8. Don't worry about knowing all the answers. If actors ask you difficult questions, help them answer them themselves as a team. If they figure out something different later on, that's OK, in fact that's great. It's flexible.

9. There is no need for a stage manager to take detailed notes of blocking, as it will flex throughout the rehearsals. New emotions, new subtext will emerge as they grow more comfortable with their character and with the process.

10. Enjoy coaching your actors. They'll be great.

Teach Actors to Create Beautiful Tableaux

What makes stage composition beautiful is the combination of many artistic factors, including the technical aspects of color and design of the costumes and sets and the lighting.

But, for this book, we concentrate on the sculpture of human bodies as they are arrayed on the stage. The positions they take, relative to each other can be as beautiful as a painting by the great masters. But, even better, they are constantly changing as characters move about.

We will concern ourselves with composing these characters in the following realms: individual bodies when they are in open spacing, and collective bodies when they are in groupings.

When characters are in open space, the individuals compose themselves with body positions, stage positions, stances, levels, and activity in ways that enhance the telling of the story by revealing character, situations, emotions, and relationships.

Groups are assemblages of two or more characters who are clustered close enough to one another that they are touching and/or overlapping so that there is no visual air space between the characters in the group. Groups create the impact of unity and are usually reserved for characters who have a common emotional or intellectual link.

Tableaux may include both groups and open spaced characters, arrayed in a manner that tells their relationship at that moment, that tells the story visually, and that decorates, or balances the stage picture with people in interesting or dynamic positions, especially when those positions are held long enough to imprint the picture on the eyes of the audience.

In free blocking we teach the actors a process that encourages them to use a wide range of positions, and to constantly monitor themselves in relation to others, such that the stage picture does not become stagnant, or repetitive. For example, in many plays and musicals, the standard position is that people stand on the stage floor. That can be boring, repetitive, and not very visually fulfilling. But simply adding the the dimension of levels, where some are standing, some are kneeling, some are sitting, some are sitting up on things, and others may be standing on or climbing on higher things makes the stage display far more visually appealing. But, in free blocking we teach and side-coach actors in many more dimensions than just level. We teach actors to use a variety of stage positions, body positions, stances, and levels. We teach them how to array themselves in the open, and in groups, including large groups, groups of two, and tight groups.

When there is a combination of arrays, and a combination of positions, all of which provide visual focus to the important person or action, and when that combination is held for a time, then we consider it a tableau, and hopefully a beautiful one. If nothing else, the tableau should add to the tone, and the drama, and the emotion of the scene.

Actors will learn those skills in the workshops in the next chapters, and they will be side-coached to apply them throughout the rehearsal process.

Chapter 6

Where Actors Move

Stage and Body Positions Create Focus

This is the first chapter in the series of Stage Movement.

Chapter 6: Where Actors Move, Stage and Body Positions Create Focus
Chapter 7: How Actors Move, Conventions of Movement
Chapter 8: Why Actors Move, Motivation

Relative Strength of Stage Position

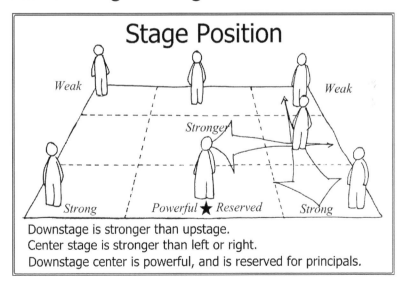

Stage position is simple to teach, yet it is a challenge to get actors to understand how to motivate themselves to use the full stage. Start with the simple, and get all actors to understand the strength of each stage position in relation to others. Most stage craft books divide the stage into nine sections: (9) up right, (8) up center, and (7) up left; (6) right of center, (5) center, and (4) left of center; (3) down right, (2) down center, and (1)down left. What is most important for creating focus is to remember that the strongest stage positions are closest to the center and closest to the front. So, center-stage is a very strong position, with only down-center being stronger. Up-left or up-right are the weakest, being furthest from the front and furthest from the center. One can argue whether down right or down left is stronger than up center, and I submit that it is a close call, and depends on lots of other variables. It is less important that we can create a mathematical formula for which fraction of the stage is the strongest, and instead, look, as a director, at the actors on the stage and determine where the focus is, and whether it is correct or should be changed.

Teach Your Actors to Change Stage Position

Set-up: Place all actors on stage and tell them to take their own space, which means to select a position apart from anyone else, collectively filling the entire stage, such that they can all see the audience, and no one is directly behind anyone else. This is the common starting position for most warm-ups and staging lessons.

Lesson: Teach them the stage positions according to their level of stage maturity. With kids who are on stage for the first time, I teach them the difference between stage right and stage left, up stage and down stage and how that downstage is stronger than upstage, and center stage is stronger than left or right.

Kinesthetic:
(1) Ask them to move, as a group, to whatever stage position you name, and do it in just 3 seconds. Go! Repeat with other stage positions.
(2) Ask them to chose as an individual, a stage position, anywhere on the stage that is either stronger, or weaker than where they are now. and get there in 3 seconds. Go! Repeat several times.

It is fun when this whole cluster of kids are running down left, up center, down right, up left, and where ever you say, kind of like Simon Says. With mixed company, adults and kids, such as in a community theater group, I run them all through the same paces.

With adults, I still run them through the same paces. Theater is kinesthetic! Get people doing things rather than just listening to someone tell them about it. With adults, or experienced people it may not take as long, but always remember, there is likely to be a novice mixed in with the group, a novice who needs the fun of running around the stage, getting confused about what is stage right and stage left, and who will be better off if he or she is part of a huddle of actors running from one space to another, and laughing along the way.

Understand the Relative Strength of Body Position

The strongest body position for pulling focus is full front. This is when an actor is positioned with face toward the audience, with the front of the body toward the audience. The weakest position is ¾ back, which is when the actor is about ¾ of the way toward full back. Some might argue that full back, or facing the rear of the stage is the weakest position, because no part of the face is visible to the audience, and as we know, the human face is the most engaging part of the body for the audience to read.

However, I believe that full back is actually somewhat strong, because it carries with it so much potential energy, as though the actor who is full back is angry, or rejecting all others, or rejected, or bearing some other emotion that is strong enough to warrant us noting the actor. Therefore full back carries with it some additional strength of focus. However, once you learn all of these principles, you become the artist, and can manipulate the subtlety of stage and body position to create interesting new lines of focus.

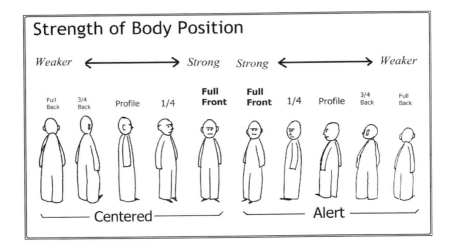

Profile, 3/4 Back, and 1/4 Front

Other body positions are profile right, and profile left, which are stronger than 3/4 back, and weaker than ¼. In short, and simplified, the closer the actor's body and face to full front, the stronger, and the further from full front, the weaker. In actuality, the position of the face, not the body, is the more powerful determinant of strength. A full front body position with the head bowed is weaker than a ¼ body position with the head up and facing full front. But those subtleties will be obvious to you as you watch for focus. Focus based on strength of body position is easy to see from the audience. Just look at the stage, and notice who has the focus. How to train actors to manipulate focus using body position will be covered later, under "Give and Take."

Not Every Theater Expert Agrees With Me. I have found at least one professor of theater who insists upon a different comparative strength of body position, including full back as a very strong position, and profile as weakest. Though I don't agree that profile is the weakest, I would enjoy hearing his reasoning. There is always something more to learn from others. Nevertheless, for the sake of simplicity, the closer the head is to full front, the stronger the position. The further from full front, the weaker the body position, with the exception of full back. Side-coach: *Give by taking a weaker body position,* or just, *Give!*

Teach Your Actors Strength of Body Position.

1. **Set-up**: Tell actors to take their own space.
2. **Lesson**: Teach them and demonstrate what you mean by each body position: full front, ¼ left or right, profile right or left, ¾ back, and full back. Teach them which positions you deem to be the strongest and weakest.
3. **Kinesthetic** – Ask each actor to assume the body position you name. Then call out body positions, one after another. Enjoy this exercise as there will be some confusion and some laughter, especially if you add "left" and "right" to the mix. 3/4 left then profile right may confuse some of them because you are referencing stage left and stage right.

Understand the Power of Levels

I also add **level** as a subset of body position. **Level is the height of the human face in the picture,** as affected by whether the actor is sitting, lying, kneeling, bending, standing, or is up on something like furniture or a platform. Notice that I did not equate level with the height of the feet. We judge level by the face. Tony in West Side Story may be climbing up the fire escape, and Maria may be leaning out of the window above him, but if their faces are at the same level, they are at the same level, regardless of where their feet are.

Actors use levels to give and take focus. The highest level is the strongest.

Again, the principle is simple, the higher the level, the stronger the body position. A person who is center, standing on a platform is stronger than a person, also at center, who is standing on the floor or sitting or kneeling, or lying down. Furthermore, a taller person, one whose face is higher, is likely to have stronger focus. If you have a short Pirate King, it might be good for him to stand on a trunk when singing, "I am a Pirate King," for example. Side-coach: *Take the stage by assuming a stronger body position,* or simply, *Take the stage!*

Men, Women, and Level. This brings us to in interesting question. Do men, who are generally taller than women, pull the focus because of the higher level of the head? I actually don't think so, but I could be wrong. The height differences between men and women may not be enough to affect focus, as there is substantial cultural acclimation to those differences, and in fact the handsomeness or plainness of the face might do more to affect focus than just the height differences of male or female.

Lesson: Teach them about levels, including the strength of body positions associated with higher and higher levels.

Kinesthetics: Say: *Explore levels by moving your body and head to a different level whenever I clap my hands. You chose the level, but eventually you should each have tried every imaginable level.* Clap your hands once every 5 seconds or so, and watch them move to various levels. Affirm their choices, and allow laughter as people get creative about how to achieve various levels.

Teach the Five Stances

Much of this book will stress how to move on stage, but ultimately, more time is spent in standing than in moving, and in plays with an open stage, such as a musical, much of the dialogue is on the open stage floor. So it is important that actors learn how to stand, or how to vary their stance according to the emotions of the moment. How to stand on the open floor, and the emotional impact of those stances, is easy to teach and learn, but do not be deceived into thinking they are not important. Standing in one of the five basic positions sends strong messages about the character and the relationship to the moment. Basically, there are five stances. Some of the qualities can be combined, creating more variations, but basically these are the five stances: (1) centered, (2) alert, (3) powered, (4) graceful, and (5) angular. Angular is usually not created on the open floor, but rather is influenced by the presence of levels, furnishings, and other props that allow the body to lean, recline, curl, drape, or stand with one foot above the other. More on the asymmetrical stance later.

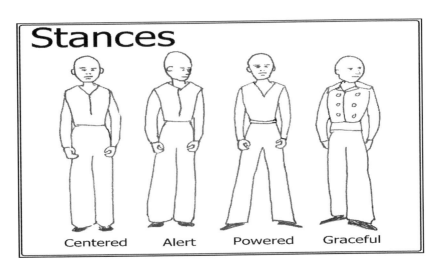

(1) **Centered** Standing in a centered position means that the head and the torso are in alignment. The nose lines up with the belly button. The centered position is fundamental, relaxed, formal, and giving. People use the centered position to listen without judgment, to speak frankly, to recede into a line of relaxed characters, and to contemplate. The centered position lacks dynamism, and as such is perfect for characters who are not yet embroiled in tension or who are thinking basically about themselves. Centered position is also perfect for warm-ups, relaxation, and self-awareness.

(2) **Alert** The alert position is when the head is turned ¼ from the torso, either left or right. The alert position indicates that the character is aware, focused, tense, and concerned about the relationship with others. Regardless of the body position (full front, ¼, profile, ¾, or full back) the alert stance tells other characters and the audience that what is happening now in the scene is important. It is dynamic, and tense, and it projects the tension out into the audience. In a musical, the alert position projects the character's deepest concerns across the apron toward the back of the house as though the character is confiding in or appealing to the silent partner, the audience.

(3) Powered The powered stance is legs apart and chest held high. The powered (or power) stance indicates that the character is strong, in control, determined, confident, and unphased by the turmoil swirling about. The powered stance is perfect for those climactic moments in a song of glory. The powered position can be combined with the alert position to indicate a moment of both tension and determination.

(4) Graceful Characters stand gracefully when they stand in a layman's equivalent of the fourth position, which is a ballet term for a foot position in which the heal of one foot is at 90 degrees (or more) from the toe or instep of the other foot, and about ½ to one full step apart. (See illustration). The graceful stance is a proper, graceful, and elegant position appropriate for gentry. Both men and women who are schooled in the arts of high society should adopt the graceful stance. This includes princes and princesses as well as their elegant servants. Dukes, duchesses, and any high-minded society people should stand in the graceful fourth position. They may be alert or centered, but seldom powered. Sidecoach: *What is the appropriate stance for your character now? Are you centered, alert, powered, or graceful?*

(5) Angular or Asymmetrical Position Angular positions are asymmetrical, creative, and natural looking. They generally explore levels that are provided by the set pieces. Imagine dividing the body with a line down the center. If the left side of the body matches the right side, the body is symmetrical. Symmetrical positions are formal and relaxed. The centered stance is symmetrical. However, when one side of the body does not match the other the position is asymmetrical. Angular positions include asymmetrical use of the arms and legs, often as they rest, lean, or touch furnishings, set pieces, or other people. Angular positions are informal and casual. They tell the story and reveal character in the moment. If your characters are informal, or are in casual or energetic situations, insist on angular positions, both in groups and as individuals. Action places characters in asymmetrical positions, too, so pose that action in asymmetrical tableau, and the story-telling of your blocking will be enhanced. I often use the terms "angular" and "asymmetrical" interchangeably when discussing body positions.

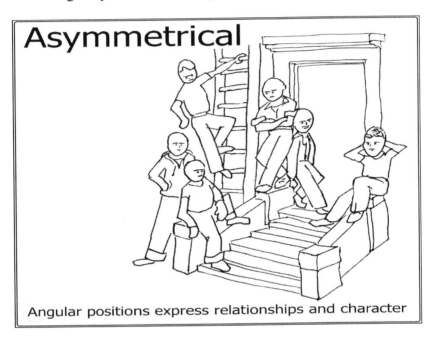

Angular positions express relationships and character

Array

When there are three or more actors on stage, there are only three fundamental arrays, (1) in lines, (2) spaced, and (3) grouped. These arrays can be combined to create full stage tableaux, or to create moments of contrast. Furthermore, the staging may flow from one array to the next as the plot progresses.

Arrayed in Lines

When characters are blocked in lines, their individuality is diminished, and the focus is on their similarity. That is good for certain situations, and bad for others. Make sure you use lines only at times when all the characters in the line are, at this moment, of equal importance. If someone becomes more important, that person should step out of the line. There are basically four reasons for arranging characters in lines. (a) The first is when there is a specification in the plot, such as a police line up, a queue, or, as in *A Chorus Line* the characters are told to stand on the chorus line. (b) Align the actors when the situation is formal, such as in a receiving line, a military formation, a choir, a formal presentation, or elegant servants awaiting the king,. Notice how that in a choir, all of the characters are dressed alike, their voices are intended to blend, and none of them is more important than the effect of the whole. For that reason, lines are acceptable. The same can be said for a military formation with rows of dragoons or yeomen or sailors standing at attention. Such a line is impressive in its totality, while each of the characters, at this moment, is less important than the total picture. (c) Use lines for certain vocal ensembles, especially in opera, when the music supersedes the plot, and when all of the characters are of equal importance. Finally, (d) use line for choreographed ensembles, especially for the corps de ballet when the image of the whole is more important than the character of any individuals.

The problem with lines is that they are restrictive. They serve an occasional purpose, but if overused, they are restrictive, stifling movement, and limiting the extent to which characters can interact, reveal relationships, and pull focus. For that reason, most of the discussion in this book will not be about arrangement in lines, but rather about the other two fundamental arrays, spaced and grouped.

Arrayed in Groups

When characters are arrayed in groups they are connected emotionally and visually. The story that unites them is displayed through their positioning and their touch. Collectively the groups contribute to full stage tableaux, and, hence, are exciting elements in the creation of beauty in composition. The free blocking director will be able to create effective groups quickly by capitalizing on the actors' own wit and stage awareness. It takes about 30 minutes of training to bring actors to the level where they can create sophisticated tight groups in less than five seconds.

There are three types of groups, (1) tight groups, (2) relating, and (3) large groups. Tight groups consist of from three to five or so characters who cluster with a linking emotion conforming to six distinct parameters. There may be several tight groups on the stage at any one time, distributed about the stage in such a way that they fill the stage, balance the stage, and create a full stage tableau. There will be considerably more training on how to create tight groups later in this book. When there are two people who are touching one another, enacting some quality of their relationship, they are relating. Large groups have the same parameters as tight groups, but generally there is only one large group on stage at a time.

Sidecoach: *Group.* or *Give me tight groups in 3, 2, 1.*

Arrayed in Open Spacing, or Spaced

The most common blocking array is spaced, or open spacing, where each of the characters inhabits a unique space on stage, touching no one else, and generally moving about from place to place without touching others or with only minimal touching such as a handshake, a kiss, a slap on the face, or handing of a prop from one person to another. Open spacing allows for excellent audience visibility and freedom of movement to express emotions and to push the plot forward. Open spacing allows for crosses, counters, and approach-avoidance maneuvers, and all the other standard movements of theater. Open spacing is the most common array for the normal comings and goings of characters who are pushing their objective and encountering obstacles along the way.

The weakness of open spacing is that it only minimally portrays relationships, and when performed on an open stage, such as in a musical or opera it generally inhabits only one level; standing. Therefore, open spacing is generally not very beautiful, is devoid of tableau moments, and eventually stagnates in its own sameness. There are only so many crosses, counters, pivots, and face-aways that can be used before the staging becomes repetitive.

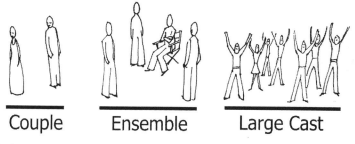

To achieve open spacing with large groups, the free blocking director teaches actors to "Take your own space." Actors should be coached to select a spot on the stage floor that is distant enough from others so that they can move freely without bumping, a spot that is not on plane with others, such that they can see the director and audience without being obstructed by someone directly in front of them, and in spots that collectively fill the entire stage. When actors take their own space, they are forming open spacing, which means that actors are arrayed in triangles, deep into the stage, and up onto the platform structures, such that each character can be seen by the audience. They are not touching each other, and there is walking space between them and they fill the depth and breadth of the stage.

Sidecoach *Take your own space.*

From *Les Miserables*

Levels, eye focus, and body positions in profile or 3/4 back give focus to the singer. The listeners are centered. The singer is powered.

Workshop 1-- FOCUS

The first rehearsal after the read through, instead of blocking the show, do a workshop on how to create **focus.**

Take Your Own Space: (2 min) Send all the actors on stage. Note how random and disorganized they look. Then give the command to "Take your own space," meaning, go somewhere where you have room to move, you can see me, you are NOT on PLANE with ANYONE ELSE, and where collectively we fill the entire stage. Repeat by having them move somewhere else, again on the command to "Take your own space," with the same parameters, in three seconds, GO! 3, 2, 1. Good. Repeat.

Teach them that this is open spacing, a great position for dance, or a big song. Compared to the random way they looked when they first went on stage, this is beautiful. And it only took them 3 seconds to get there. And the stage is well balanced. We will use this command often.

Stage Position. (3 min) Teach actors the relative strength of stage positions. Downstage is strong, Upstage is weak. Stage left and Stage right are weaker than stage center. Down center is the strongest spot on stage. Send them as a group to a variety of weaker, or stronger places on the stage. (UL, DR, UC, LC, etc.) Then later, don't call out a place, rather call out a relative strength, such as stronger, even stronger, very weak, etc. The quicker the better, so they end up running around the stage having fun. End with the command, "Take your own space."

Body Position. (3 min) Teach actors the relative strength of body position. Full Front is Strongest. 3/4 back is weakest. 1/4 front, or sharing is common for conversation. Profile is good for arguments. Full Back is weak, but looks ominous. Then call out body positions and have them turn to each, FF, FB, 3/4 B, Profile, 1/4 Right, 1/4 left, etc. Then call out a relative strength, and have them select which position they will move to.

Level. (3 min) Teach that the higher the head, the greater the strength, the lower the head, the weaker. Levels range from lying, sitting, kneeling, bending, leaning, standing, and standing on something. (Let infirm or immobile actors make their own decision about what they can do) Tell them to stake a strong level, then a weaker one, then weaker, then weaker, and so forth till everyone is lying down. Reverse it until everyone is standing, or standing on something. Mix it up a bit. The faster, the more fun. Finish with "Take your own space. "

Stance: (3 min) Demonstrate the five stances, (1) centered, (2) alert, (3) powered, (4) graceful, and (5) angular. Call out for them to stand in each stance. When they get to angular, encourage them to use a different level, such as sitting, kneeling, reclining, leaning, or to freeze in a dramatic pose in response to an emotion you call: scared, hiding, celebrating, confronting, sneaking, concentrating, relaxing, cheering, etc. Finish with, "Take your own space, CENTERED"

Focus: (1 min) Teach that focus is making the audience see the person who is speaking, or some prop or business that's important. We create focus with the strengths we've been learning, also by eye focus, and by movement. Eye focus, means look at the speaker. Point to and/or call the name of different individuals around the stage and ask the cast for eye focus on that person.

Give and Take: (5 min) Teach that *take* means to take the stage, or take a stronger position than anyone else when it is your turn to speak. *Give* means to take a weaker position than the speaker when you are not speaking. The fluid change of focus on stage is a matter of constant give and take.

Activity: If you have a large cast, sit half of them down in the house to be observers. It's important that they see how powerfully the focus shifts. Say to the ones on stage, "Take your own space." Next, as I point to you, take the stage. All others, give. Point to one at a time, and let others weaken. Remind them they can weaken with body position or level or eye focus. For now, they cannot move to a different stage position. Point to everyone at least once. Ask the "audience" where the focus goes.

Switch the observers and actors and repeat. End with, full cast "Go someplace new and take your own space."

Chapter 7

How Actors Move
The Conventions of Stage Movement

This is the second chapter in the series of Stage Movement about how and where the actor moves in order to reveal emotions and to shape the focus.

Chapter 5: Where Actors Move, Stage and Body Positions Create Focus
Chapter 6: **How Actors Move, Conventions of Movement**
Chapter 7: Why Actors Move, Motivation

Share

When two people are facing each other in a 1/4 body position it is commonly referred to as the **sharing position**. The sharing position is a standard position for dialogue between two standing characters. Most of our fundamental movements will make reference to moving to and from the sharing position, although I am not convinced that the classic sharing position is particularly effective. I would rather people moved in response to the emotional thrust of their character rather than to simply assume a classic blocking position.

Sidecoach: *Share.*

Sharing is the standard position for dialogue. Each person at 1/4, facing each other.

Face Away

When two characters are onstage but one is facing away from the other, we call that **facing away**. Imagine that Sarah is talking with Gonzo in a sharing position. He says something that annoys her and she pivots away. They are now both ¼ position facing in the same direction. He is looking at her back or shoulder, and she is looking away. That is facing away, or the face away position. One can easily move from facing away to a sharing position simply by turning or pivoting. Face away will be discussed more fully as an extension of Approach-Avoidance.

Sidecoach: *Face away.*

Crossing to face away is a dynamic movement, part of the flow of approach-avoidance in dialogue.

Pivot

A quick way to give or take the stage is to pivot, which means to turn in place A character who is weak because of facing upstage can quickly take the stage by pivoting to face full front. Or, as in the illustration below, a character who is strong can weaken suddenly, giving focus to an upstage character, by pivoting in place. A graceful pivot keeps one foot on the ground, sort of like a pivot foot in basketball. One may also pivot gracefully from a 4th position, right to left, or left to right by keeping both feet on the ground and pivoting on the balls of the feet.

Teach the Sharing Position and Facing Away

1. **Set-up**. Pair up the actors. Note: Here is one of those opportunities to randomize the groupings. I recommend that you have people pair up with someone they would not normally select. For example, say: Move to the other side of the stage and pair up by putting your arm around the shoulder of your partner. Now pair up with some one else. Now pair up with someone else. At this point it should be rather random. If there is an even number of actors, the pairing is easy. If there is an odd number, the odd person should pair with you. Also notice that I asked the people in the pair to touch by putting their arm around the shoulder. That is for two reasons. (1) It becomes visually clear immediately who is and who is not paired, and (2) it begins the process of teaching actors to touch. You will see later in the exercises on tight groups that touching is important to beautiful blocking. Ask the pairs to decide who is A and who is B (or Andy and Bobbie)
2. **Lesson**: Demonstrate what you mean by (a) taking a sharing position and (b) pivoting to face away. Then pivot back to a sharing position.
3. **Kinesthetic**. Tell Andy and Bobbie to take a sharing position. Then tell Andy to pivot away. Then tell Bobbie to pivot away. Then tell Andy to pivot back. Then Bobbie, and so forth. Get them to move by pivoting into sharing positions and face away positions, quickly and easily. If you feel like stretching them, ask them so say any phrase they want as they move as long as Bobbi's phrase includes the word "Why" and Andy's includes the word "Because." Then let them decide on their own whether they will pivot to a sharing position or a face away position as they say their "Why" or "Because" line. Let Andy and Bobbie trade the "Why" and "Because" line and do it a few more times. Switch partners randomly, and repeat. Instead of "Why" and "Because" try "When"

and "After," or "How" and "It's Easy." Enjoy the laughter as actors create little stories to go with the lines. But keep the focus on appropriately motivated pivots to share or face away. After awhile you will notice that the actors begin to motivate their pivots to reflect the emotion of their lines. That is exactly what we want to generate --movements that are motivated by emotions.

Movement

The fundamental stage movements are (a) the cross, (b) the pivot, and (c) the counter. The cross includes the downstage cross and the upstage cross. For simplicity, we consider a cross directly across the stage to be done the same was as a downstage cross. For free blocking to be effective actors must master these three movements to such an extent that they flow naturally, in much the same way that a basketball player has practiced dribbling so much that she can dribble around obstacles without so much as looking at the ball. Dribbling must be so deeply ingrained in the skill-set that it appears to happen naturally, and so that the basketball player can focus her attention on other things, such as who is cutting, where the defensive player is, how much time is left on the clock, and so forth. To the actor, the crosses, pivots, and counters should flow just as naturally, as the result of constant practice. Here are the principles of effective crosses, pivots, and counters.

Teaching Stage Movement: To teach these movements, put the actors on the stage, ask them to take their own space. Describe and demonstrate each movement, then ask the actors to do it themselves, simultaneously.

Cross

The cross is a movement, usually a walk, (but not necessarily – it could be a run, or a saunter, or a crawl) from one position on the stage to another, generally in a direction across the stage. A cross is motivated by a desire to get somewhere, a destination, or to get away from someone or something. Some destinations are habitual, such as the refrigerator, the couch, or the bathroom. Some are inspired by the objectives of the character or the circumstances of the play. Never should a cross be unmotivated or aimless.

The Graceful Cross: A graceful stage cross has specific parameters. If the actor is not skilled enough to perform a graceful cross, or if the character is not a graceful character, then it is OK to do a simple cross. A graceful cross is an odd number of steps, three, five, or seven (occasionally 9 or 11). The cross begins with the upstage foot, which is the foot that already extends in the direction of the cross. The cross ends with a step by that same foot. For example, If an actor is standing in a 1/4 position (sharing position) facing left, her upstage foot is her left foot, and her left foot is slightly ahead of (stage left of) her right foot. If she wants to make a three step cross to her left, she begins with her left foot, step one. Then her right foot, step two. Then her left foot, step three. She should end in the same position as she began, in a 1/4 left position. If she wants to make a 5 step cross to her left, she simply adds two more steps in the middle of that sequence, but the beginning and the end are the same. Start with the upstage (leading) foot, and end with that same foot.

The beauty of a well-practiced graceful cross is in the economy of movement. Feet don't shuffle. One begins, moves, and ends on balance. One begins from a sharing position, and ends in a sharing position. In contrast, do that same cross with an even number of steps and you will notice that the actor finishes in a 3/4 back position, rather than a sharing position. The easiest cross, one that should be practiced first, is the downstage cross, meaning the actor's movement takes her downstage and across the stage, at an angle, such as from up right to down left. Side-coach: *Motivate a graceful cross.*

Simple Cross:
Yes it is graceful and economical if the cross uses the precise number of steps, and begins and ends on the proper foot as described above. However, rather than getting too fixated on how many steps, or whether one starts or ends with the correct foot, it is more important that the cross feel natural, and within the movement parameters of the character. It is OK to do a simple cross, which is nothing more than a motivated movement across the stage, regardless of which foot is the lead foot, how the feet end, or whether it takes an odd or even number of steps to get there. So, practice the graceful cross. But, until it flows easily from the actor's body no one should be too fixated on the precision. A character who is excited should cross with excitement, regardless of the number of steps. A character who is aged and walks with a cane or walker will move differently. A character who is tired should walk like a tired person. A lover should run like a lover. A child should play like a child. A shuffler should shuffle. A wanderer should wander. Movements should always flow from the emotional and physical parameters of the character at that moment in time. Learning to make graceful and economical crosses is simply enhancing the available physical tools for the actor.

Side-coach: *Cross.* Or, *Motivate a simple cross.*

Cross in Front

The cross in front is a variation of the downstage cross. Cross in front of (downstage of) and beyond another actor. Be careful not to stop directly in front of the other actor, as that creates an awkward situation. Continue crossing until you have walked past the other actor. When you get to the end of your cross, you can stop in a position that faces away from the other actor, or you can pivot back to face the other actor. Don't pivot until after you finish your line.

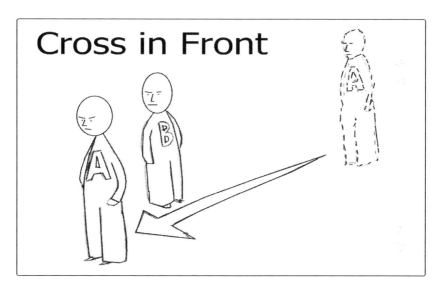

Cross To

Another variation of the downstage cross is the *cross to,* where you cross to the other actor. If that actor is facing you, you end up in a sharing position or in profile facing one another. If that actor is facing away from you, you come up close to his or her shoulder, and find yourself in a **face away** position. Another variation on the *cross to* is the *cross to* followed by a *cross away*. That means, you cross to a character, perhaps speaking angrily and forcefully, but as you finish your line you walk past or away from that character and end up facing away. The *cross to,* followed by a *cross away* is a particularly effective cross combination for a person who is angry or exasperated.

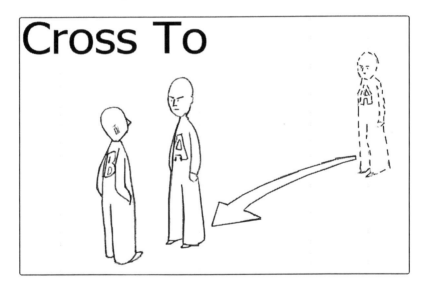

Cross Away

Cross away is a third variation of the downstage cross. Cross downstage while moving away from the other character, instead of going toward or in front of that character. You will end up on the other side of the stage from the other character. When you get to the end of your cross, you may either pivot to face the other actor, or remain facing away. Again, do not pivot until after you finish your line. If you remain facing away you have the opportunity to pivot on a later line, or to pivot when you have a particularly strong reaction to something another character says.

Open Up

Opening up is a form of pivot, a graceful, economical movement that turns the body by swinging one foot back. For example, stand in a sharing position, then open up that position by swinging your downstage foot backward until you are facing full front. When you open up, you strengthen your body position, and may be taking the stage. Opening up is a graceful way to take the stage without much movement.

Sidecoach: *Open up.*

Cross and Pivot

Now combine a cross and a pivot. Starting upstage left, take a five step downstage cross toward stage right. Stop. After stopping, pivot to face the right. Then take a five step downstage cross toward stage left. Stop. Pivot. Cross left. Stop. Pivot. Cross right. Continue this practice until you're down stage as far as you can go. Then go back upstage, and practice it some more. Better yet, use an **upstage cross** to get you there.

Side-coach: *Motivate a cross and pivot.*

Turn

To turn is a more natural way of pivoting. When one turns, both feet lift from the floor and are repositioned, but the body stays generally in the same place, just facing the other way. If you are not comfortable with the ease of the pivot, or of opening up, or if your character is not the kind to pivot, or if your character is not in the disposition to pivot, simply turn.

Cross Upstage

The upstage cross is a sweeping arc. The goal is to walk upstage but to end up in a 1/4 position, a sharing position. Notice that if you just walk from the downstage to the upstage in a straight line, you end up facing upstage, which is a rather awkward direction to be facing. It is more graceful to start walking toward the upstage in an arc that brings you to a stop in a ¼ front position. Generally the upstage cross swings in an arc along with a corresponding change of speed. The actor starts off quickly, even running, and slows gradually before coming to a stop.

Side-coach: *The composition has moved too far downstage and needs an upstage cross from someone. Please motivate an upstage cross.*

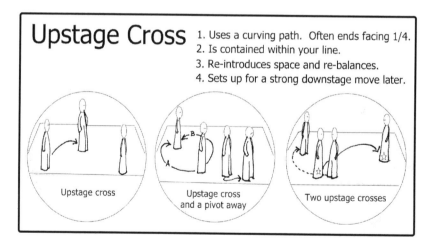

Purposes of the upstage cross:
(1) An upstage cross can also be used as a set-up for a strong move that comes later. (2) It can be used to weaken a character, provided the crosser ends in a weak body position, usually 3/4 back. (3) An upstage cross can also be used to rebalance the stage, or (4) to add variety to the blocking. For example, if there have been a series of downstage crosses the actors find themselves moving closer and closer to the front of the stage. To re-shift the position to the upstage again, take an upstage cross. You are then in a great position to make a strong downstage movement on a strong or important line.

Side-coach: *In order to strengthen your next line, you need to set it up with an upstage cross.*

When do you move on the upstage cross?
You begin to move just prior to speaking your line. An actor speaks through the cross and stops moving at or before the end of the line. If the line is too short to correspond to the full time it takes to make an upstage cross, divide the line into two parts. Say the first part before or at the beginning of the cross, then walk (or run) and say the remainder of the line at the end of the upstage cross.

For example, if the line is "Momma, Daddy is home," the first word, "Momma," might be said at the beginning of the upstage cross, as the character begins to run to the window, and "Daddy is home" can be said from the upstage window at the end of the cross.

Side-coach: *Leave part of the line for after you finish the upstage cross.*

Counter

The counter is fundamental to cooperative staging. The counter is a move in the opposite direction made by a second actor in response to a downstage cross by the first actor. The principles of an effective counter are as follows:

1. Make a counter move when an actor makes a downstage cross in front of you.

2. To counter, you cross in the opposite direction of the original cross. Begin your counter just as the crosser passes in front of you.

3. The counter should travel less than 1/2 the distance of the original cross. For example, a 7-step cross should be countered by a 3-step counter.

4. At the end of your counter, pivot to face the actor who made the original cross.

5. Begin the counter move after the cross begins, and end the counter before the cross ends. In other words, the counter move is contained within the time of the cross, and does not extend beyond the time of the cross on either end.

6. The motivation for a counter is to see and hear more closely. Therefore, the actor making the counter should be focusing his eyes and ears on the actor who made the downstage cross.

7. Only one actor counters. If the crosser passes in front of two or more other actors, only one of them counters, usually the first.

Side-coach: *When an actor crosses downstage of you, remember to counter,* or, simply, *Counter.*

Sweeping Turns

The sweeping turn is a variation of the upstage cross, kind of a condensed upstage cross, and consists of a sweeping outward turn executed with quickness and energy that repositions the actor upstage of another character. The sweeping turn is a higher level skill, as it looks great but feels awkward to the amateur actor, because the move begins by turning away from the intended target. Amateur actors want to move toward the person they are speaking to, whereas the sweeping turn begins with a move away from the target, then continues in a 180 degree arc, swinging back toward the target character at the end of the arc.

Sidecoach: *Approach with a sweeping turn.*

SWEEPING TURN

The sweeping turn is a condensed upstage cross, a sweeping outward turn that repositions the actor upstage of another character.

For example: Star finds himself downstage of A and B, but needs to greet one of them.

If he makes a direct cross to B, he squeezes between, and bumps them. Not good.
If he makes a direct cross to A, he is facing upstage. Not good.

His best move is a SWEEPING TURN, either to A or to B, that begins by actually walking away and then arcing back to them from slightly upstage.

Avoid Parallel Crosses

Never allow two actors to cross in the same direction at the same time. It's a parallel cross, and it doesn't look good. On the other hand, there are always exceptions. For example, a parallel cross may be used for comic effect. There is a parallel cross in the Broadway staging of *Phantom of the Opera*, when two impressarios read a letter from the Ghost, and it is funny and gets a chuckle. Two clowns sneaking into a high status space may move parallel. Mr. Serious might follow Mr. Clown upstage and out of Mr. Clown's sight, in a couple of parallel crosses. It would be funny. But generally, don't do parallel crosses.

You may be tempted to allow a parallel cross if one person is chasing another, such as Hopeful Lover is pleading with Hard-to-Get. When Hard-to-Get crosses away, you may think Hopeful Lover should follow her. But no. Wait until she gets there. Wait until she stops. Then, it is alright for Hopeful Lover to cross to her. However, here's another exception: if the scene is a farce then Hopeful can follow Hard-to-Get all around the place. But, generally, don't allow parallel crosses.

Which leads to the next, and very important staging principal, one character moves at a time.

One Character Moves at a Time

This is a principle that is very important. Move. Then stop while the other character moves. It's a form of give and take. But even more so, it drives the energy of the focus from one character to another in a pace that is quite striking. The faster the movement and stop, the more powerful the increase in pace and tension. Always reinforce with your actors the principle that only one character should move at a time. This principle also has many exceptions. First, lets acknowledge the exceptions. (1) The gracefulness of a well-timed counter move is an exception. (2) Dancing and choreographed movements are exceptions. (3) Re-arranging large groups is an exception. (4) A reaction that everyone shares in common is an exception, but be careful of this. If there is a character who responds differently from others, that person should have his or her personal moment of reaction. (5) Mirrored comic movements can happen simultaneously. (6) Couple or group entrances and exits, such as in an encounter, are are exceptions and I include in this the planned chaos of a chase scene. (7) High speed pacing of a high tension moment leading to a tension freeze can include simultaneous movements. But, given those exceptions, try your darndest to manage the movements to happen one at a time. If you train actors well to follow this principle, your story telling will be enriched, the subtext will project, and there is better control over the pace.

Movements can be tiny, such as the lifting of the head, or covering one's mouth, or dropping the jaw. They can be mid-sized, such as pivoting in place, or lifting a gun, or pouring a drink. Or they can be large, such as a downstage cross, leaping onto a treasure chest, a run and stop, or running into your lover's arms. But regardless, the principle remains, that only one character moves at a time. Let's examine a simple scene as an example:

Example 1: **The kissing scene:** It may seem natural that a couple choosing to kiss one another should be an exception to the principle that one character moves at a time, especially considering that there may be no lines spoken. After all shouldn't they move toward one another and embrace simultaneously? Maybe. But imagine it this way, one movement at a time: As they stand apart she throws out her arms; he then puts his arms out, too, as he looks around to see if anyone is watching; she then runs to him and wraps her arms about his waist pressing her cheek against his chest; he then gulps as he assesses what is happening; she looks and notices that his arms have not wrapped around her in return and she reaches out and pulls one of his arms in around her waist; he hesitantly wraps his other arm around her waist and breathes heavily; she then lifts her head, eyes closed, and lips pursed, waiting; he purses his lips too, and turns his head to one side, then the other, as if to figure out where to put his nose; and so forth. Notice when the movements are separated that the subtext is exposed. She is taking control, and he is frightened about doing it wrong. Relationships, pecking order, status, motivations and internal struggles are all given voice. The separated movements create focus on the important actions and reactions. Exaggerate those movements and problems and you have farce. Keep them earnest and you have drama that may also be humorous.

The same principle of one movement at a time keeps the blocking crisp.

For example, in this scene, notice how only one character, She or He, moves at a time:

Example 2. **The bitter scene.** She spits, "I hate you!" and spins to cross away where she stops, arms crossed and shivering in disappointment.

"But Bindy" he appeals, as he takes one step toward her, his hands wringing his navy cap.

"Don't call me that!" she screams, spinning to face him, her chest heaving with tension, "Its 'Rebekkah' to you. A Jewish name."

He shakes his head, stunned, struggling to find the right words. "I...I didn't mean anything by it."

She runs at him like she wants to slap him, but he cowers and she passes by, crying. "You wouldn't even know," she snaps as she grabs a glass vase from the table and freezes, contemplating her next move.

He moves upstage and around as though to get into her line of vision, "Bindy...uh, Rebekkah, I think I can learn, if I just knew what I said wrong."

She spins, holding the vase, ready to throw. He stops. "Get out! She says as she points to the door. He steps toward her but stops as she lifts the vase higher and says, "Out!"

Get the point? One person moves at a time, usually in concert with their spoken lines, but sometimes in response to to emotional impulses from the subtext. The one-person-moves-at-a-time-strategy brings tremendous focus to your scene. This one concept alone can strengthen your play beyond that of many other directing strategies. Try it. Remember there are exceptions, and don't make it be too rigid, but, this is, after all, a play, and you are responsible to control what the audience notices.

Sidecoach: *One person moves at a time.*

Sequenced Freezes

At first thought, a group reaction seems like it should happen with simultaneous movement. A scream in the dark, a gunshot, a thunder clap, a power outage. All of those things project a moment of reaction that could easily happen simultaneously. Fine, if there are no characters with different status, subtext, or motivations, but we know that is not true. Find a way for the important and separate reactions to happen in sequence. The playwright will help you with the sequence, for the dialog immediately following the stimulus will suggest how to sequence the reactions.

For example, in *The Music Man* Tommy Djilas sets off a firecracker during the 4th of July speech by Eulalie Shinn. The assembled crowd must react as if, well, as if a firecracker were set off in the room, but then they must hold a tableau of their reactions as the reactions of the key players reveal themselves. First Mrs. Shinn reacts as though she has been shot (particularly funny if the oversized shotgun Amaryllis has been toting happened to point at her. If that is how it is played, there needs to be a moment of reaction for Amaryllis. Tommy Djilas reacts with delight and an escape. Gracie Shinn points a finger at Tommy as the culprit. The Constable captures Tommy, and so on. It's probably wise to give a reaction moment to the Mayor, whose ceremony has been disrupted and whose wife has been "shot."

The key point is that the reactions must proceed in a sequence of movements and freezes that allows the focus to shift to the key characters as they reveal their individual responses. They can move very quickly, but they should still be in a sequence, and should not be a mass of confusing movement. It is highly important that the audience see what the director wants them to see.

As a facilitative director you are always looking for ways to achieve order without being controlling. An easy way to achieve this flow of focus is that people move whenever they are inspired by the stimulus, but they freeze in their reaction. The motivation for that freeze can be shock. Those freezes will automatically happen at separate moments, after their individual reaction, and that also creates a sequence of freezes, hence a sequence of reactions. S*ide-coach: React within your character, then freeze.*

Use Stock Blocking Patterns Occasionally

Certain moments on stage lend themselves to stock blocking. I teach you these not to require you to block your characters, but to be aware of how your blocking affects the audience. In other words, the audience reads the blocking, and understands what is happening. If your free blocking does not discover effective patterns for these stock moments, then you may wish to side-coach your actors to approximate these stock patterns for the sake of expediency. These stock patterns include swinging your face toward the audience, and the exit line, as well as five types of encounters, (1) the chance encounter, (2) the unwitting introduction, (3) anxious hunter finds the missing person, (4) hopeful lovers, and (5) business as usual.

Swing Your Face Toward the Audience

The audience deserves to see the actor's face whenever anything important is happening. If the actor is reacting, speaking, or getting ready to do something, make sure that facial expression is visible to the audience. This often requires the actor to make a downstage turn, or some kind of a turn that sweeps the face toward the audience. For example, if Big Actor is facing upstage, giving focus to someone else and she hears startling news, she must motivate a turn that displays her facial reaction to the audience. Perhaps she can check-in with someone standing behind her, using that as a motivation to swing the face toward the audience. Perhaps she can motivate an avoidance move that swings her face toward the audience. Perhaps she can make an upstage cross, which swings the face toward the audience.

Tony Award Winning Actor Nathan Lane is skilled at making just such sweeping turns, making his facial reaction visible to the audience. For example, Nathan knows that if he is facing away from the speaker when startling news is heard, he is then set up to make a sweeping turn of his face, through the downstage, until he is looking at the speaker. He saves that move for his funniest reactions. Pre-Broadway actors awkwardly find themselves giving reactions to the back wall of the stage. Or they turn their back to the audience as they turn to move. Teach them to make that move so it swings the face toward, or through, the audience.

Deliver an Exit Line from Near the Exit

Characters are generally given the last line to speak before they exit. That line is their exit line. It is generally good blocking practice to have that actor deliver the line at or near the exit, to avoid a long silent walk to the exit after the line. Long walks after the exit line interrupt the pacing of the scene, especially if the other characters must wait for the exiting character to be out of ear shot before they continue. Teach your actors to set up their exit line by being at the exit door or the wings before they being their exit line. Or teach them to use the exit line to time their exit so the line finishes just before leaving the stage. Teach them to avoid saying a final line then crossing the stage in silence or crossing the stage to exit as another character has begun to speak. There are exceptions, especially when using a moving tableau which I describe later in the book, but generally, deliver the exit line from near the exit.

Stage Encounters

Often on stage people meet other people. These encounters require movements that clarify for the audience whether the characters were expecting to meet one another. For this section, I will be describing some very particular movements for the staging of encounters. They are precise movements that work for various situations. This may appear to be the antithesis of free blocking, but it is not. You as a director need to know how certain moments on stage are most easily blocked, and encounters require a certain amount of staging. They can still be free blocked, meaning the actors can make decisions about where they enter, how far they walk, what their motivation and subtext might be, and what lines they use to accomplish the staging. Furthermore, the other characters on stage are required to weaken themselves to create focus. All of those are free blocking decisions.

Here are several types of encounters, together with an explanation of the best movements to clarify for the audience what type of encounter it is: (1) Chance Encounter, (2) Unwitting Introduction, (3) Anxious Hunter, (4) Hopeful Lovers, and (5) Business-as-Usual. There are, of course, other types of encounters, and it should be easy to use the principles provided here to help you invent movements that accentuate the relationships in those encounters.

1. The chance encounter. When characters have a chance encounter onstage, meaning that one or more of the characters is not expecting to meet the other, they should enter from opposite sides of the stage and/or pass each other. During the pass one or the other will notice and call to the other, and they will turn to meet and greet. This is important, for otherwise the encounter will appear to have been planned. Remember, movement must tell the story to an audience who are reading visual cues as well as dialogue cues as to what is happening. If it is a chance encounter, it should not look planned, and if it is a planned encounter, it should not look like chance. The key element is that the two walk past each other before they turn to speak. The turn should be downstage, sweeping the face toward the audience. Pre-Broadway actors tend to swing their face upstage, so watch closely and sidecoach the downstage swing of the face.

For example, in *The Music Man*, Harold Hill unexpectedly runs into his old partner in crime, Marcellus, in a chance encounter on the street. In this case Harold and Marcellus should enter from opposite sides of the stage, pass each other, and in the passing, they notice each other and turn to face each other, followed quickly by their lines and a handshake. It is the passing, the recognition, and the turning back to each other, even with double takes if appropriate, that makes it clear that it is a chance encounter.

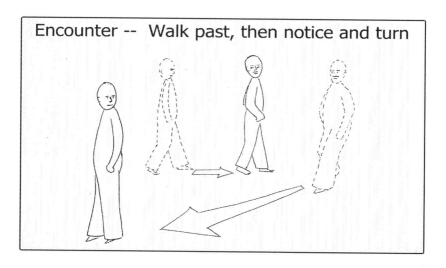

2. The unwitting introduction. The unwitting introduction is an encounter where one of the two, the introducer, wants to make verbal contact with an unwitting person. The introducer should approach the unwitting from behind, or should cross as in a chance encounter, such that when he/she ends up behind the unwitting person, forcing the unwitting person to turn to face the introducer when his/her name is called. Again, this should be a downstage turn, swinging the face toward the audience. When the unwitting person turns to face the introducer it reads clearly to the audience that the unwitting person did not at first know or recognize the introducer. For example, in the Music Man, Harold Hill leads into his famous patter song "Ya Got Trouble," by calling Mr. Dunlop by name. Though the two are strangers to each other, Hill has deduced Dunlop's name from the fact that he came out of Dunlop's Grocery. Whether you stage it that Dunlop is working in, at, or around the store, or whether Dunlop is leaving the store, what is important is that Hill comes up behind him or crosses to behind him before he calls out to Mr. Dunlop by name. As Dunlop turns to face Hill, the introduction reads clearly to the audience as an unwitting introduction.

3. The anxious hunter finds the missing person. When one character, the anxious hunter, has been searching all over for a missing person, the missing person is usually onstage, downstage, and the hunter enters quite rapidly, crossing on an upstage plane, getting almost past the missing person before noticing the missing person. The hunter stops immediately then delivers the "I've been looking for you" line while moving downstage toward the missing person.

4. Hopeful lovers. Hopeful lovers reveal a great deal of attraction through their movements. Often the attraction is only in the subtext, as the text may be about something superfluous or obtuse. Lovers, or hopeful lovers, encounter each other, with hope in their hearts at opposite sides of the stage. Think of it as the realization of the scene described in "Some Enchanted Evening" from Rogers and Hammerstein's *South Pacific.*

Some enchanted evening, you may see a stranger,
You may see a stranger across a crowded room
....Then fly to her side, and make her your own
Or all through your life you may dream all alone.

One, in this example the woman, is already onstage, or enters first and stops, waiting, but momentarily looking away. The man enters quickly and stops, or slows to a stop, upon sighting the woman. She turns quickly to face her hopeful lover. And they both stop where they are, looking at each other. That set of movements, the quick entry and stop, followed by the quick turn and stop, calls the audience attention to the two lovers at opposite sides of the stage. This works if there are only two people on stage or if the stage is filled with a party of people who give. It is the movement, combined with the rest of the ensemble giving, that focuses the attention where it belongs. From there, depending on the dialogue and subtext, the lovers can either run to each other, or stand apart for some time, staring at one another, or they may look away from each other with embarrassment and follow that with stolen glances. Or they may engage in some sort of repartee that draws them inexorably closer. Or the woman may act coy, working around the stage as the man watches, and as she notices him watching. Regardless of the dialogue the initial encounter is best staged with the precisely timed movements of the hopeful lovers.

5. Business-as-Usual. Often characters encounter people they already know, in situations they are familiar with. In that case the movements should be accompanied by simple activities that indicate business as usual. The characters may glance at each other, but basically focus on going about routine tasks. For example, when boss arrives at the office in the morning, secretary may hand her a cup of coffee, take her coat, and give her the day's agenda for perusal, all as if it had been done this way every workday for the past several years, regardless of the content of the dialogue. When the dialogue introduces a problem, the business as usual abruptly stops. Or, for example, when Charlie arrives at the bar after work, bartender hands Charlie his usual draft, throws the usual bowl of popcorn in front of him, and asks him how things are while turning to continue washing and drying some glasses, conducting business as usual. When Charlie discloses startling news, business as usual stops abruptly. In the business-as-usual encounter, keep the business simple, common, and nonchalant. Business-as-usual encounters obviously work best if the characters have props to manipulate, and can include mundane activities such as picking up and scanning the mail, putting groceries away, picking up the mess left from last night's party, pouring a cup of coffee, or any activity consistent with the place of the encounter. The key is that the characters engage in mundane activities, barely noticing one another, until such time as the dialogue reveals something startling.

Set Up for Important Movements or Entrances

If you want to have your lead character run to center stage for an important confrontation, then you must set up that character at great enough distance away, up left or up right, so there is room to run and so that the run is in a down stage direction.

If a character is to make an important entrance from Up Right, then you must set up by having that entrance be open, and uncrowded. Other characters should be out of the way. (Unless, of course it is important to have the way blocked, as part of the story.)

If the Pirate King is going to leap onto a treasure chest to sing, someone needs to set that chest there, and the Pirate King needs to have a route to get to the chest without stumbling over people.

These are examples of blocking that sets up for a particular, important move to come later. Blocking, in the traditional sense, anticipates the important plot moments, and makes sure the characters are set up in a place where they can make their move gracefully.

Workshop 2
MOVEMENT

Review the workshop on Focus, quickly and completely. (1 min) Say: (1) Take your own space, (2) Go to a stronger place on stage. (3) go to a weaker place, (4) take your own space, (5) assume a weaker level, (6) a stronger level, (7) take a weaker body position, (8) weaker, (9) stronger, (10) Take your own space centered, (11) go somewhere else and take your own space powered, (12) stand graceful, (13) stand alert, (14) stand angular in a pose that expresses wild desire (or any other emotion), (15) stand centered, (16) give eye focus to (point to someone), now (17) give if I am not pointing to you, and take if I point to you. Do not cross. (Point to several people.)

Stage Movement: Say, "Pair up by putting your arm on someone's shoulder." (any extra person pairs with you). "You will work as partners for a few minutes, then you will pair with someone else." Have them introduce themselves and shake hands. Have them select one as "Hero" and one as "Buddy."
Say: I will demonstrate a movement. You will repeat the name of the movement as you do it. Don't move until I say GO.

Sharing Position: Say: Hero and Buddy, stand 1/4, facing each other and say, 'sharing position.' Go.

Face Away: Say: Hero, pivot away, like this, and both say, "face away." Go.

Sharing Position: Say: Hero, now pivot back and both say "sharing position." Go.

Face Away: Say: Buddy, pivot away, and both say, "face away." Go.

Sharing Position: Say: Buddy, pivot back and both say, "sharing position." Go.

Face Away and Share with Dialog. Demonstrate, then assign Hero and Buddy to Share or Face Away as they alternate improvised lines. They can say whatever they want as long as their line starts with either "Why" or "Because." This can be fun, but notice how the *face away* ups the emotional tension. Let all pairs do it at the same time.

Cross: Teach that *cross* means to walk somewhere across the stage. Upstage cross means to go upstage, and a downstage cross means to go downstage.

Cross in Front: Say: Hero, make a downstage cross in front of Buddy about five steps, and stop facing away. Say "Cross in front." Go.

Cross to: Say: Buddy make a downstage cross to Hero, stopping in a 1/4 position right beside hero. Say, "Cross to." Go.

Sharing Position: Say: Hero, pivot back to face Buddy in a 1/4 sharing position. Both say, "sharing position." Go.

Cross Away: Say: Buddy, turn and do a downstage cross away from Hero about 5 steps. Stop in a face away position. Say, "cross away." Go.

Upstage Cross: Demonstrate that an upstage cross is an arc, sweeping wide, and beginning in the opposite direction from where you will end up facing. Say: Hero, make an upstage cross, arcing to the spot you originally started from. Say, "upstage cross." Go.

Upstage Cross. Say: Buddy, make an upstage cross, arcing to the spot you originally started from, and end in a sharing position with Hero. Say, "upstage cross." Go.

Repeat the entire sequence of crosses, starting with Buddy this time. Cross in Front, Cross To, Pivot, Cross away, Upstage Cross, Upstage Cross, back to the beginning. Saying each term as you do it.

Crosses with Dialog. Demonstrate then assign Hero and Buddy to move on alternating improvised lines, using crosses in front, crosses away, face away, pivot, sharing, and upstage crosses. They can only move on their own line. The line must start with either, "How" or "It's Easy." This will be fun. But if you have a large cast, have half of them be audience. Stop them after they've used lots of crosses and pivots and face aways. Then switch them out.

Thanks: Say: Thank your partner by name. Tell them something you like about what they did.

Switch partners, pair up by hands on shoulders, introduce and shake, select a hero and buddy, and do the entire sequence again, beginning with the pivots and face away, all on your command. When you get to Crosses with Dialog, tell them they can say anything they want, but their phrase must begin with, "When" or "After."

When finished, say: Thank your partner by name, tell them something they did that you like, move to a new place on stage and "take your own space."

Counter: Demonstrate a counter. Teach, when a person crosses in front of you, you counter, which means walk a little in the opposite direction, looking at the crosser, and stopping your counter before they finish their cross.
Say: Pair up by hands on someone's shoulder. Introduce and shake. Appoint one as hero and one as buddy. Stand about 8 feet apart from your buddy. Don't move until I say go. Then hero, make a downstage cross in front of and past buddy, saying "cross in front." Buddy, you will counter, and say, "counter." Go. Repeat a few times, giving each a chance to practice countering.

Chapter 8

Why Actors Move
Motivation

This is the third chapter in the series of Stage Movement about how and where the actor moves in order to reveal emotions and to shape the focus.

Chapter 6: Where Actors Move, Stage and Body Positions
Chapter 7: How Actors Move, Conventions of Movement
Chapter 8: Why Actors Move, Motivation

"Give and Take" is a Powerful Concept

The principal of **Give and Take** is simple: On most lines (though not all), the **speaker moves, and takes a stronger position than any other actor on stage.** (Takes the stage) And simultaneously, every other actor assures that he or she is in a weaker position than the speaker (Gives) It is as simple as that. It's all a matter of give and take. Take the stage when you plan to speak. Give when it is not your turn to speak. This creates a flow of focus from one character to the next, and is particularly important when there are more than two characters on the stage at the same time.

Most actors understand that they should take the stage, but it is amazing how many actors do not know when, or even how to give. They have not learned the art of collaborative staging. That is why we teach them, and practice these principles regularly. For example, a particularly head strong actor I know would take every opportunity to stand on the stage full front. No matter what his blocking, he would eventually work his way into a full front position and keep it. He was sending the subliminal message, "I am important, and every reaction I give to every other character is more important than what other people do." Perhaps you know one of those amateurs. A person like that creates havoc with focus, and must be reminded to give. A graceful 3/4 back, with the head turned profile, or a graceful profile with the head turned to 1/4 is much more beautiful and it allows others to move in and out of focus as the script demands. Furthermore, when Actor Big needs focus, he or she can pivot slightly just prior to a line and as a result the line is more powerful than if there was no strengthening movement to precede it.

Side-coach: *Take the stage. Remember to give.*

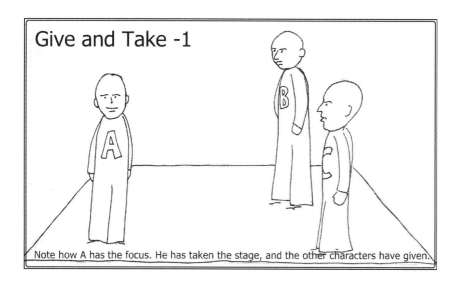

The complexity comes in the infinite variety of stage positions and body positions that actors can be in at any one time.

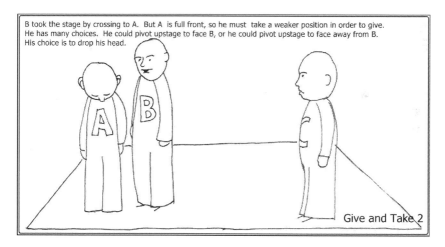

The nice thing about free blocking is that the director does not have to refine the position of every single actor on stage. The director simply reminds them, through side coaching, and the actors themselves will make the proper adjustments.

When actors take the stage they must take a stronger position than any other actor, and in so doing they manipulate the three principles of stage strength, (1) stage position, (2) body position (including levels), and (3) movement.

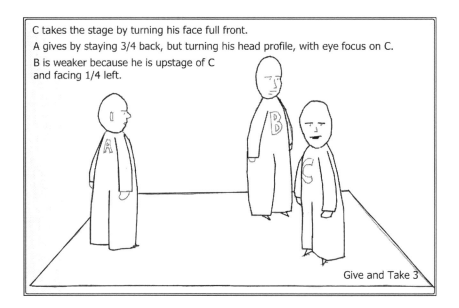

Notice in the illustrations that it is clearly visible to the audience which character has the focus. The changes of strength of body position are simple, but effective.

Sidecoach: *Give. Take.*

Teach Your Actors to Give and Take

Set-up: Divide the cast into two groups, one to observe as audience, and one to be on stage.

Lesson: Explain that the actor who takes the stage must take a stronger position than any other actor, and that means that the others must give by taking a weaker position. Remind them that they can use body position, stage position, levels, movement, and eye focus to strengthen or weaken themselves.

Kinesthetic: Tell the actors on stage to take their own space, which means to select a position apart from anyone else, collectively filling the entire stage, such that they can all see the audience, and no one is directly behind anyone else. This is the common starting position for most warm-ups and staging lessons.

Tell the actors on stage that you will point to one person (or call that person by name). That person is to take the stage by moving to a stronger position, and all others are to give, by taking a weaker position. Then point or name each person, one at a time, giving the others time to react. I sometimes also ask that person to say one of their lines, or to say a stock line that I provide.

Ask the observers to confirm whether or not the focus goes to the correct person, and if not, what could be done to correct it. Make the corrections, and use those as teachable moments.

Then send the other half up on stage and repeat the exercise.

Applaud for each group.

Motivate Movements by Approach-Avoidance

When there are two or more characters in dialogue there are only two basic blocking movements, either (1) toward the other character, or (2) away from the other character. That is it. Toward, or away. Approach, or avoid. Of course there is an infinite number of variations of those two movements, large movements, tiny movements, up stage or down, quickly or slowly, and so forth, but, for the sake of understanding how actors learn to motivate their own movements, keep it simple. Either approach or avoid, toward or away. (In comedy, there are parallel moves, and in dance there are lots of parallel moves, but ignore those for the moment, as this concept is about dialog, not about visual comedy or dance.)

Left to their own choice, without side-coaching, most amateur actors will stand on stage delivering their lines without moving anywhere. But standing still in a semicircle of talkers does not reveal much about the inner struggles, nor does it engage the audience who have come to watch a play, not just to listen to a play recitation. Therefore, the concept of traditional blocking fills that void, and the director tells actors where to move, and what motivates that move. However, in a free-blocked show, actors must learn to motivate their own movements, and to create movements that vent the inner conflicts, the struggles, the desires, and the fears of their character.

The Psychology of Approach-Avoidance. Let's examine those two basic movements from a psychological and motivational perspective. Again, there are two basic movements in dialogue, (1) movement that approaches another person or desired object, and (2) movement away from, or in avoidance of another person or object. That is it. Either you approach, or you avoid. I have borrowed a phrase from psychology to describe the two basic movements and their motivation, *approach-avoidance.* As a psychological term approach-avoidance describes the motivation to move closer to something that is desirable only to have the potential negative consequences of contacting that desirable object tend to push one away. Imagine that the desirable object is to go sky diving, which from a distance seems intensely thrilling and appealing. However, the closer one gets to actually jumping out of the plane, the stronger the fear. The desire motivates the approach, and the fear of consequences motivates the avoidance. The interesting feature of approach-avoidance is that the further one is from the object of desire, the feelings, both positive and negative, are less strong, but the positive has a way of dominating. In other words, you are attracted to the goal in spite of small misgivings. The closer one gets to the goal, the more powerful all the feelings, but especially the negative feelings, the fear, the worry, the uncertainty. The bride or groom who has cold feet at the wedding is experiencing approach-avoidance. The wedding seems a desirable goal, in spite of small misgivings, but the closer one gets to saying "I do" the stronger the fear becomes. This reveals a truth about humanity, that we fear what we desire.

Approach-Avoidance Motivates Characters to Move. Characters in plays have goals. They have desires. They are striving to get somewhere, to be with someone, to accomplish something. However, the closer they get to their desires, the more they encounter their fears. The closer their approach, the stronger their tendency to avoid. Approach-avoidance are powerful motivators for movement on stage. Motivating an approach is simple. Walk toward the person you are addressing. An avoidance is more subtle, because it expresses an inner fear, a worry, an uncertainty, and it motivates the character to move away, or past, or to turn away from the other character.

For the sake of this discussion, we will use approach-avoidance more broadly than just as a description of psychological conflict. For the stage, any movement that is motivated toward another character will be called an *approach*, and any movement that is motivated away from another character will be called an *avoidance*, or as I sometimes call it, simply a *move away*.

Approach movements are straightforward and generally easy for actors to motivate. When a character speaks to another, he or she tends to look toward or to move toward that character. Good. That is an approach. If the heroine is trying to convince her friend to join her in a scheme, there is an approach motivation. If the friend is intrigued by the scheme, that is also an approach motivation. It's simple. If your goal involved connecting with another person, there is a natural tendency to approach. So I will not spend much time on approach moves, except to say that two characters cannot continue to approach one another *ad infinitum*. They will run out of space. One of them must eventually motivate an avoidance movement. One of them must walk away. If one walks away, then we can begin again with a series of approach moves. Therefore, lets think more about how to motivate avoidance, how to walk away, how to reintroduce space between two characters in dialogue who have been moving toward one another.

First, let's remember some basics about stage movement: (1) Only one character moves at a time. (2) Each character begins moving just before his or her line and may continue through much or all of the line (taking the stage). (3) The character then stops, weakens, and remains still as the other character speaks (giving the stage). The movement to take the stage can be subtle, such as the lifting of the head, or it may be strong, such as a strong downstage cross.

Subtextual Phrases that Motivate Avoidance

The most psychologically sound motivation for an avoidance movement comes from an introduction of fear, doubt, or uncertainty. If the text of the line is indeed about fear, doubt, or uncertainty, then, by all means, use it to motivate an avoidance movement. However, even if the text of the line is an expression of certainty, the subtext can express doubt. Here are some subtextual phrases that can motivate avoidance.

1. I'm not sure how best to say this…

2. I'm not sure I completely trust you…

3. "I'm worried that we're getting ourselves into trouble…" For example: The line may be, "Johnny, I love you," which looks like an approach line. But if you introduce uncertainty, she may say, "Johnny, I love you," as she turns her back and walks the other way. Suddenly the subtext intrigues.

4. I'm afraid…

5. I'm not sure I agree with what you're saying…

6. I'm not sure I agree with what I'm saying…

7. I'm thinking about someone who is over there somewhere.

8. I'm remembering...

9. I wonder...

10. I'm looking for something.

11. I'm looking at something or someone else in the distance.

12. You disgust me.

13. I'm uncomfortable with the feelings I have with you right now.

14. I'm scheming. I'm forming a plan that I may or may not explain to you.

15. I'm so excited I can't stand still.

16. This is a big beautiful world and I need space to express my thrill.

17. I don't want you to see my face right now.

18. I don't agree with what you're saying.

19. I'm angry at you.

20. I hurt terribly, and I need to be left alone.

21. I'm hiding something.

I'm sure you can think of more, and when you do, add them to this list.

Avoidance moves are graceful and intriguing. They come in several forms, the most common being: (1) simply turn and face away from the other character, (2) walk past the other person and stop in a face-away position, (3) turn and walk away from the other person, then either stop in a face-away position, or end by turning back to face the other.

Side-coach: *Motivate an avoidance move,*
Sidecoach: Phrase one of the avoidance motivations as an evocative question: *Are you hurting? Are you hesitant? Are you afraid? Are you thrilled? Are you scheming? Are you hiding something? Use that feeling to motivate an avoidance move.*

Short Runs

One of he most powerful, and oft neglected movements is the short run. The short run consists of a motivated run, followed immediately by a motivated stop.

Sidecoach: *Motivate Yourself to Run. Motivate Yourself to Stop.*

The stage is of limited size. Unless your set and interpretation is flexible, you cannot run across an open meadow on stage. You cannot chase the burglar through the entire neighborhood on stage. You cannot run to the top of the entire mountain. The graceful actor begins those movements, with all the enthusiasm of the entire chase, climb, or run, and then interrupts the move before reaching the edge of the stage. I call this movement a short run. Begin to run as though you had the desire to run forever, then interrupt yourself with another thought, and pull to a stop, a stop that contains both the desire to continue the run, and another stronger, conflicting idea which forces you to stop.

For example: Imagine the line is, "Mother, don't jump off that cliff!" The line motivates a run toward mother. But, rather than running off stage into oblivion, the actor runs toward mother who is somewhere off stage, then halts quickly, still terrified about what mother will do, but with an interrupting thought in the subtext, such as, "Since I can't reach her in time, what shall I do now?" or "I must get someone to help," or, "This is a disaster that will give me a heart attack." Whatever the subtext, it is enough to motivate a stop, an interruption of the original run. A common motivation to stop is the desire to exercise self control in an otherwise out-of-control world. The stop contracts the run into a movement that carries the full emotional impact of running, while containing it within the limits of the stage space.

Usually the motivation for the run is less dramatic than catching mother at cliff edge (I just made that up), and, subsequently, it is more easily interrupted by a conflicting subtextual thought. Such motivations to run are generally (1) a sense of urgency, (2) an expression of a thrill, (such as being in love or anticipating something wondrous) (3) a desire to convince someone else, (4) to escape a troubling situation, or (5) to escape a troubling thought. Lets walk through each of those, with examples.

(1) A **sense of urgency** is a great way to motivate a short run. Look for urgency whenever you can. Urgency thrives in plays. Plays thrive when there is urgency. Your challenge as a free blocking director is to help actors find the urgency and to express it through movement.

Side-coach: *Do you feel urgency? Can you motivate a short run?*

For example, in *Romeo and Juliet* the illiterate servant asks Romeo for help in reading the list of invitees to Capulet's party. Romeo reads him the list of guests and quizzes the servant about who is hosting the party, then the servant shuffles off to invite them. But, imagine how much more fun that would be if the servant feels an urgency to go invite all those guests before he forgets them, only to be called back by Romeo to answer a question. He starts to run off again. Romeo calls him back to another question. The servant's urgency to do his master's bidding conflicts with his desire to be grateful to Romeo for reading the list. He comes back, answers again, then runs even more quickly, afraid he'll forget, only to be called back again. This could happen several times, raising the angst of the servant, and amusing Romeo and Benvolio and the audience. Short runs reveal urgency and angst. And, as in this case, they can turn a small character bit part into a memorable moment.

Many plays have an urgency at the climax: the police are coming, the bomb is about to go off, Lancelot is about to rescue Guenevere from being burned at the stake, Harold Hill must escape before being captured, etc. But there are also many urgent moments within the play: In Romeo and Juliet alone there are many moments of urgency: to exact revenge, to escape, to be with one's lover. Each of those moments can abide a short run as an expression of urgency, shortened by a wisp of self control.

(2) **Thrill**. Sometimes the motivation for a contracted run is because of a thrill, or the anticipation of something wondrous. How many songs in musicals are about being in love! Those thoughts of love motivate movement. A short run is preceded by envisioning the object of desire. That visioning lifts the head up, the eyes outward, and the body into a forward lean, until the desire to reach the image bursts forth into a short run toward it. Side coach the actor to run toward that thought, to run toward the wondrous thing or wondrous idea.

Side-coach: *Can you envision that? Motivate a short run toward that image.*

The lyrics of the song will suggest the images. Envision, then run toward the imagined lover, envision and then run toward the anticipated joyful reunion, envision and then run toward the beautiful life, envision then run toward the dream. But, interrupt that run with the realization that it is only a dream, or that perhaps there is another beautiful image in the other direction, or that you have reached the imagined lover, who wraps you in his or her imagined arms. Envision the wondrous, then run toward it, and just as quickly motivate yourself to stop.

You will see those movements in a love song, when she runs up onto the porch, looking out toward where her lover is expected. She stops herself, and grabs the porch post, leaning back as though she is dancing with the imaginary lover. She spins around, then later she runs toward the beautiful life she envisions together with him. Then she motivates a stop by imagining the beautiful world all around her, as she whirls in place to enjoy it.

Get it? The short run, including the motivated stop, motivates the actor to explore the entire stage with bursts of energy separated by pensive moments and graceful changes of pace.

For another example, "Everything's up to date in Kansas City" from *Oklahoma* is not just declaratory, it is a country boy bragging about his thrilling experiences in the city. Side coach the actor to envision all those beautiful things, to run toward them, and to stop himself with motivations like, "Of course I've got Kansas City all figured out, so I'm not THAT impressed," or "Don't you think I'm pretty hot stuff for having been to the big city," or, "I could tell you more, but you'll have to pull it out of me" or, "I can't say more because it would be embarrassing," or any other subtextual motivation that the actor discovers as he works through the song. First envision the wondrous object, then run toward that vision, and then interrupt that run with a contrasting subtext.

(3) **Convince Someone Else** Another motivation for the short run is to feel a desire to convince someone else. In that case the short run should be toward the other person. In a song there may be several people, or groups of people scattered about the stage who the character has a desire to convince. A short run toward one group, followed by a graceful moment of gesture, followed

by another short run toward another group, followed by another graceful moment or gesture can define much of the movements in a song such as "Kansas City," almost without the need for a choreographer. In fact, if you are directing the show without the help of a choreographer, use strategies like the short run for some of your musical numbers. (See Runs and Poses)

(4) **Desire to Escape a Situation** A desire to escape a troubling situation or troubling thought can motivate a contracted/short run. In the classic comic operetta, *The Mikado,* Pooh Bah nervously tells Koko that "The Mikado is approaching the city and will be here any minute!" This announcement puts Koko in deep trouble, at risk of having his own head cut off because, as Lord High Executioner, he is under the Mikado's orders to execute someone at once, and the next in line for execution is himself!

He has the desire to escape the troubling situation. He could run. But, of course, he has no where to hide. He could run, but his partners need him to save their necks as well. He could run, but he has an idea for a ruse that would please the Mikado, if they can pull it off. The free blocking director would side coach Koko to want to escape, to run, but to motivate his own stop, to interrupt himself (as there is more of the scene that needs to be played out). Run to save his own neck, run to hide from the terrible news, run away from his reality. But, interrupt his run with any subtextual idea that works for him, such as, "Tell me more" or, "What are we going to do?", or, "Just give me a minute and I'll think of something" or, "I don't know where to go as there is no place to hide."

Such a run, and stop, followed by a pivot, and more runs and stops brings a motivated, high energy pace to a climactic comic situation. The audience will more quickly connect with the urgency of his dilemma, with his subtextual struggle if he is moving, and motivating his own stop, than if he just stood there dumbfounded. The contracted run gives vent to powerful emotions and allows the audience to connect with the urgency of the situation for that character.

(5) **Desire to Escape a Thought**. Sometimes the character is motivated to a contracted run by a desire to escape a thought rather than a situation. For example, to find out that a loved one has just died may motivate a character to back away then turn and run, as though running away from the terrible thought. Of course, the actor must then interrupt that run, and stop. Motivate the stop with an internal struggle to stand and face the problem, or to look to others for help, or to be confused as to what to do next, or to regain self control, or any other effective and conflicting motivation.

Back Away Then Turn to Run.
When running to escape a thought it is graceful and effective to begin that run by backing away, followed by turning to run, followed almost as quickly by a motivated stop. Often, the stop calls attention to the tension that has arisen in the breath. The character may find himself breathing fast and shallow, an extension of a terrible internal tension.

The sequence of action to back away then turn to run is:

(1) begin to back away from the overwhelming thought,

(2) turn to run from it (leading with the head), then

(3) stop quickly, motivated by a contrasting thought, and

(4) hold that tableau while the quick breath expresses the continuing tension.

Sidecoach: *Back away then turn to run, but motivate yourself to stop.*

Rhythm

Rhythm is the pace, the change of pace, and the contrast of pace in adjacent moments within and among scenes. Sometimes the pace is slow. At other times it moves quickly. At others it is ascending (common) or descending (hopefully rare) or it stops abruptly. The rhythm of a play is affected both by the pace of the dialogue and by the pace of the movement. The most common pacing is to grow in tempo and intensity throughout a scene until there is an emotional outburst, an emotional peak, a decisive action, or a startling discovery, at which time the dialogue stops abruptly. There is a moment of tableau and tension, and subtextual struggles within the characters. Then a character breaks, and moves, and the pace begins anew at a somewhat lower level of intensity. Some manner of partial resolution has relieved the tension temporarily, but only temporarily. The pace will rise again. That pattern of rising to a peak, abruptly stopping, then starting again at a lower level of tension is the beat cycle, or simply, a beat. Some theatrical folks refer to the "beat" as the moment of silence that follows the peak, before action or dialog begins again. That's OK. In film they call the beat cycle a sequence, followed by a beat. Use whatever term you want, but remember, there is a rhythm of repeated cycles of building toward climactic moments, with quickening pace of movement, quickening dialog, and rising resolve of the protagonist, usually accompanied by rising stakes. One of my old college directors used to click a stick rapidly on a chair back to indicate that the pace should be increasing. It was his form of sidecoaching.

Sidecoach: *Increase the pace.*

Tone

Tone is the emotional effect of movement and staging. Is the movement threatening, or jovial, or anticipatory, or worried, or violent, or sympathetic, or playful, or hopeful? These are emotional states that should be reflected in the pace, rhythm, style, clustering, and contrast of the movements. It is not enough for a character to stand in the corner being worried. Being worried is internal, and is invisible to the audience and to other characters. To bring that emotion to the fore, to create tone, there must be associated movements, groupings, gestures, and most importantly tableau.

Relate

Relating is a subset of grouping, and generally consists of only two characters in the group. When actors relate, they position themselves near to or touching someone with whom their character, at this moment, has a relationship. Their positioning and business portrays something about the relationship, and about the attitudes of those characters at this moment. The business could be something like putting groceries away together, playing video games together, washing and wiping dishes together, pouring a drink, giving a back rub, arm around a shoulder, leaning a head on a shoulder, or anything that is consistent with the characters and the text.

In large group scenes, when characters are asked to relate, the dyads of actors collectively use the entire stage, with much open space, and with as much asymmetry and use of levels as can be justified within the context of the relationships. The important characters take positions downstage or center, and atmosphere characters take positions at the periphery. There can be considerable movement within and among relationships. Some actors may be standing alone. Still others may be in tight groups, and others may be in couples, triads, or quads.

Side-coach: *Relate.* Or, more completely: *Place yourselves in a position near to or touching someone with whom your character, at this moment, has a relationship. Use business to show that relationship.*

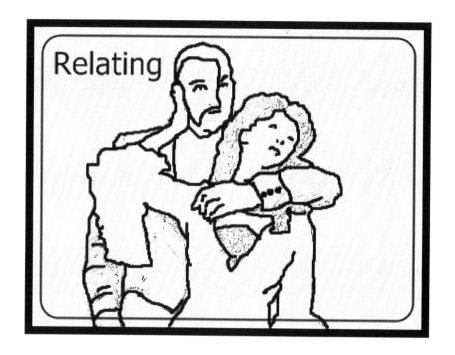

Relating also works well in small scenes, with just the principals. When alliances shift, or relationships become strained, the characters move apart. But it is impossible to show a shifting alliance if there was no visual alliance to begin with. When one character comforts another, relate. When one character helps another, relate. When one character feels connected emotionally to another, relate. When two characters are on the same side of the argument against a third, they should be together, relating. If the situation changes, so should the grouping. When two characters represent the same concept, or the same occupation, they should relate (two cops, two clowns, two students in the principal's office, and so forth. That doesn't mean people are always touching or relating, but neither should people stand at arms length for the duration of a scene because you need stage picture to contribute to telling the story, and relationships are part of that story.

Sidecoach: *Relate.*

Teaching your actors to relate will be covered in the section on forming tight groups. In fact, relating can be considered a two-person version of a tight group.

True Story about the Power of Relating. Indulge me a personal story. I was acting in a show, rather late in my career, long after I had written the bulk of this book. My character was the old guy. I had one solo which I sang to my granddaughter. The director gave me blocking and gestures that amplified the lyrics, which I dutifully did. But to me, something important was missing. I felt a need to relate to this girl, like a grandfather, so for a moment I broke from the proscribed gestures and moved over behind her and absentmindedly ran my fingers through her long hair, as though it was something we had done when she was a child. Her character liked it and it relaxed her in a moment of stress. Long story short, when the four weeks of six-sold-out shows-a-week finally ended, there was a review in my back pocket from the local critic who said the show was mundane except for a "surprisingly tender" song in Act II.

My point is that when you take the time to relate, it trumps well planned gestures every time.

Workshop 3 - MOTIVATING MOVEMENT

Review the previous workshops.
(1) Take your own space, centered in 3, 2, 1, Stand centered, alert, powered, graceful, and angular.
(2) Take the stage if I point to you. Give to whoever I'm point to, but don't cross. (Point to several)
(2) Form a group with 3-5 people, heads at different levels, heads toward the center, with no visual air space between people, balancing the stage, with the emotion, WALKING A GIANT DOG, in 5, 4, 3, 2, 1 Freeze.
(3) Pair up with someone new by holding shoulders, start in a sharing position, and improvise a dialog where you move every time you speak, making sure you both get to pivot to face away, cross in front, counter, cross away, and an upstage cross to a sharing position, each sentence must begin with either "Why" or "Because."

Subtext Teach: Characters seldom say what they really mean. To get at those hidden meanings look at the circumstances in the play. Who is secretly in love? Who is afraid? Who is scheming? Who is unsure? The quick way to unearth subtext is to assume that everything a character says masks an opposing feeling. "I Love you" may mean, "I want I love you, but I'm afraid." Fear is the subtext. Audiences love to figure out the subtext. Feed them some.

Approach-Avoid Teach, there are only two movements, approach or move away. Motivating approach is easy. **But you can't approach on every line; someone must move away to open up the blocking**. Use a subtextual conflict to motivate a move away. I will give you some to practice with.

Say: Pair up, by putting hands an shoulders. Select a hero and a buddy. Take a sharing position. Select one of your lines, and say it to your partner, Hero first, followed by buddy. Go.
Say, This next time, motivate a move away before you say that line, either a pivot to face away, a cross in front, a cross away, or an upstage cross by saying the following line under your breath first. After your line, then pivot back to face your partner, hence giving, so they can do an away move.
1. I'm not sure how best to say this...
2. I'm not sure I completely trust you...
3. I'm worried that we're getting ourselves into trouble...
4. I'm afraid...
5. I'm not sure I agree with what you're saying...
6. I'm not sure I agree with what I'm saying...
7. I'm thinking about someone who is over there somewhere.
8. I'm remembering...
9. I wonder...or I have an idea.
10. I'm looking for something.
11. I'm looking at something or someone else in the distance.

12. You disgust me.
13. I'm uncomfortable with the feelings I have with you right now.
14. I'm scheming. I'm forming a plan that I may or may not explain to you.
15. I'm so excited I can't stand still.
16. This is a big beautiful world and I need space to express my thrill.
17. I don't want you to see my face right now.
18. I don't agree with what you're saying.
19. I'm angry at you.
20. I hurt terribly, and I need to be left alone.
21. I'm hiding something.

Struggle with That: Teach: Don't worry about figuring out all the subtext. Just struggle. Let your body, hands, and feet feel the struggle. Move somewhere. Subtext will emerge. One simple struggle subtext is "I don't want to admit this."

Demonstrate then say: I'll give you a line and you repeat it straight. Then, say it on your own, struggle with it. For the sake of the exercise, struggle so hard that you almost never finish the line. We'll do about 10 lines.
1. You're right. I am a big fat liar. - Music Man
2. I've grown accustomed to her face -My Fair Lady
3. Empty chairs and empty tables, now my friends are dead and gone. --Les Mis.
4. You want to change the world? Change your mind first. -Kinky Boots

5. Who could ever learn to love a beast? - Beauty and the Beast
6. I don't know how to love him, what to do, how to move him. --Superstar
7. Who has the right as master of his house to have the final word at home. - Fiddler
8. If you were gay, that'd be OK, I mean, cuz, hey, I'd like you anyway. --Avenue Q
9. Let me be your shelter. Let me be your light. You're safe. No one will find you. -Phantom
10. No more gazing across the wasted years. Help me say goodbye. - Phantom
11. Stay with me and hold me tight and dance like its the last night of the world.-Miss Saigon

Short Run with Motivated Stop: The short run adds dynamism to the play at crucial moments. Demonstrate, then say: Imagine you've just heard horrible news. When I say go, turn and run away toward stage right about five steps, really hard, then stop yourself with the subtext, "I can face this," gather your breath and pivot back. Go.

(2) Thrill: Demonstrate, then say, Imagine you're in love and you envision your love. When I say go, run toward stage left, really hard as if to get that imagined lover, five steps, then stop yourself with the subtext, "I'm in his/her arms right now" wrap your arms around yourself and turn in place. Go.

(3) **Escape a Situation.** Demonstrate then say: Imagine your character feels like "I gotta get out of here!" Turn and run toward stage right, then stop with the subtext, "Oops, where do I go?" Then turn and run the other way, and motivate your stop with the subtext, "What's wrong with me, calm dawn." You can make noises or talk to yourself. Go.

(4) **Escape a Thought**. Sometimes characters are motivated to run to escape a thought or painful news. Example: Jack finds that his mother died. He runs with a desire to escape the pain of that thought. He motivates himself to stop He might motivate the stop with an internal struggle to stand and face the problem, or to look to others for help, or to be confused as to what to do next, or to regain self control. This time you decide your own motivation to stop and turn back.

(5) **Urgency.** Something has to be done quickly. Demonstrate, then say: When I say Go, imagine, "I've got to tell the Mayor before the train leaves. There's the whistle!" Run to the right, hard, five steps. Motivate yourself to stop with, "I've got a better idea." and turn back. Go.

(6) **Back Away and Turn to Run**. Hear shocking news? Don't just stand there. Follow this sequence: React, back away, turn the head away, then follow and run 3-5 steps, then stop, usually leaning or holding on to something, breathe, and gather yourself.

Review: You have learned to motivate your movements with approach-avoidance subtext. And to use a short run with a motivated stop when your character feels urgency, thrill, or the need to escape a situation or to escape a distressing thought.

Chapter 9

Groups and Tableaux
The Beautiful Elements of Composition

Grouping is my trademark. I'm proud to have developed these techniques, and to share them with theater companies and directors who want their staging to be beautiful. Take some time to really understand and apply this chapter. Your work will transcend function and achieve the status of art.

Tableau

The tableau is a moment of story telling through body positions that is both beautiful and dynamic and that is held long enough to imprint the image on the audience.

There are two forms of tableau, a full stage tableau, and a character tableau.

Character Tableau

A **character tableau** (sometimes called a pose or a suspended gesture) is a moment in the action usually between two characters, that deserves to be sculpted into beautiful or dramatic poses that tell the story and show the relationship at that moment.

For example, in *Les Miserable* there is a character tableau when Eponine dies in the arms of Marius as they sing "A Little Fall of Rain," and much of that song is tableau, with the dying girl draped across the arms of her beloved. Do an image search on Google and you will see how powerful that visual moment is, how it tells the relationship, and how the tableau is maintained long enough to imprint it in the minds of the audience. It has been impressed in my minds eye for 25 years, so it must have been effective.

Sometimes, however, the character tableau is for a fast movement. For example, a slap is a fast movement that is difficult to tableau, but since it is important, probably a plot changing moment, it deserves a tableau. So, the tableau should come immediately <u>after</u> the slap. The tableau will be the moment when the impact of that strike is held in a dynamic, beautiful, story telling position, long enough for the impact to be imprinted. She slaps his face and instantly regrets it. He rolls his head with the punch, grabs his cheek, looks at her incredulously. Tableau that moment. Hold it. It emphasizes the slap, lengthens the impact of the slap, and imprints the emotional reaction to the slap for each character in the minds of the audience. The same can be said of a moment of terror, a kiss, the giving of a gift, and even a pie in the face. If the moment is worth remembering, it deserves a tableau.

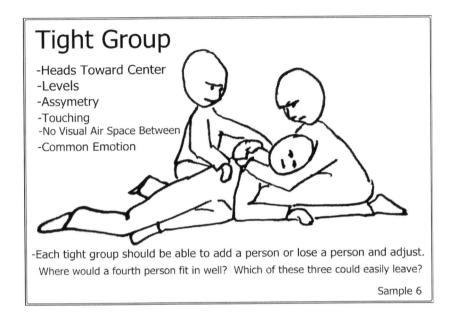

Full Stage Tableau

The **full stage tableau** is a well balanced moment that includes principals and others. It usually includes some characters in groups, others taking their own space, and some or all in poses that tell the dramatic story. In otherwords, it is a full stage picture, beautifully shaped and balanced, with levels, character, groups, and a character tableau.

Directors must help the actors identify those moments of potential tableau and to hold them. Here are some tips.

First and foremost, whenever two people touch each other, or touch the same object at the same time, hold that moment. Also, encourage the actors to find those moments when they can touch, for actors tend to live on the stage in a force-field shell, repelling all others, unless you as the director encourage them to express their relationships through touch. Side-coach: *Touch another character whenever you can.* or simply, *Touch him (her).*

For example, a handshake should last long enough for us to see who is dominant, who is awkward, who is hopeful, who is lying, or whatever the dynamic is. Hold that handshake, and let us imprint the relationships. A handshake should never be just a perfunctory greeting. It has depth and subtext. Hold it as a tableau. Side-coach: *Hold that tableau as long as you can.*

Another example: Giving a gift, or handing a prop from one person to another is often a moment when relationships change, when energy flows from one to another, or when a plot point needs to be impressed. Hold that moment. For example, in the play, *The Silent Bells*, the prince gives a crown to Anne-Marie, a crown that symbolizes wealth, and that will be an important gift to the Christ Child in the creche at Christmas. There is subtext in the relationship between the prince and Anne-Marie. Passing the crown from one person to another should be savored: she still on her knees before the prince, his robes flowing, her hands reaching up, his hands reaching out, and the golden crown between them as she hunts in his eyes for an explanation for his generosity, and whether there is any attraction between them. Savor that moment, and let the audience savor it. I am not suggesting that there be silence. For indeed the dialogue can continue, with perhaps a beat of silence. But hold that tableau. Placing of a birthday cake, accepting an engagement ring, a soldier giving his photograph to a girl before he leaves for war, Grandma passing along a keepsake to Granddaughter, handing a piece of incriminating evidence over to the police, moments like these are filled with subtext, and the tableau should be savored.

In a musical, tableau moments often coincide with orchestral accents or lyrics in the songs. Actors learn to strike the tableau in time to the music, but the director must remind them of the need for tableau at important moments.

Remember, the tableau is a moment of story telling using relational body positions that is both beautiful and dynamic and that is held long enough to imprint the image on the audience. The full stage tableau is often a combination of spaced individuals and groups and includes suspended gesture. Examples of suspended gestures are when, in the climax of *West Side Story,* Maria clasps the dead body of her beloved Tony to her breast and spits the words, "Don't you touch him!" The full stage tableau includes not only Tony and Maria down center, but the entire ensemble of Jets vs. Sharks gathered round in asymmetrical groups on a variety of levels, as well as Officer Krupke and Doc, taking their own space, helpless on the outskirts of the tableau.

Side-coach: *Hold that tableau moment as long as possible. Imprint it.*

Full Stage Tableau

From *Light in the Piazza*

Think in Static Pictures

A director who is concerned with creating effective composition is wise to think visually in static pictures, almost as though you were staging a series of dramatic group photographs. At each moment of the play there should be an image that we can remember. In a free-blocked show it is up to the characters to create those images, and it is up to the director to teach them how, and to side-coach them when they forget.

Side-coach: *Groups! Provide Focus! Tell the emotional story through your body position.*

I have found that it is very difficult to get actors to understand how long they can hold a tableau. My rule is: **Hold the tableau as long as the dialogue allows:** Note that I did not say to hold the tableau only as long as it is mentioned in the dialogue, or only long enough to accomplish the task implicit in the tableau. Hold it as long as possible.

For example, a very funny moment in Gilbert and Sullivan's *The Mikado* is when Koko, Pooh Bah, and Pitti Sing throw themselves at the feet of the Mikado, the Emperor of Japan, in terror, afraid for their lives because they have mistakenly executed the son of the Emperor. It's a topsy turvy situation that can't be explained here, but needless to say it gets great laughs. Keep that tableau as long as possible. Amateurs might be tempted to bow to the emperor, then stand right back up, but no, keep that tableau, as it is dynamic, it shows a relationship, and it will bring laughs with every variation, and believe me there are lots of variations such as people starting to get up, people bowing lower with every painful threat, people blaming one another, pushing and shoving (and rolling), all while still bowing prostrate.

Stop on the Stairs

In normal life stairs provide a means of transition from one level to another, such as from first floor to second, or from ground level to the front door. However, on stage, stairs provide much valued levels. Variety in levels helps create tight groups, enhances the focus, and helps make all the actors visible to all of the audience. Rather than using stairs to transition from one level to another, actors must be encouraged, and reminded to use stairs for positions. Don't just go down the stairs, stop on the stairs. Don't just go up the stairs, stop on the stairs. Maybe stop with one foot up. Maybe stop and lean against the rail. Stop and sing a phrase of your song from the stairs. Stop and relate to someone who is on the step just below you. Form a group with people on various levels of the stairs. Sit on the stairs. Lean back on the stairs. When making a grand entrance down a set of stairs, stop at the top, then stop part way down, and savor the power that the elevation grants you. My experience is that actors need encouragement to break the habit of traveling up and down on stairs, and to think of the stair case as their friend. To free blocked actors, the stairs are like a magnet, drawing the actor toward the creative potential for positioning. To other actors stairs are just a troublesome barrier that must be negotiated with caution for fear of falling. Sidecoach your actors to *Stop on the stairs* and you will find them unleashing the power of the staircase.

Sidecoach: *Stop on the stairs. Go up onto the stairs.*

Groups

Groups are assemblages of two or more characters who are clustered close enough to one another that they are touching and/or overlapping so that there is no visual air space between the characters in the group. Groups create the impact of unity and are usually reserved for characters who have a common emotional or intellectual link. For example, a cluster of people hiding under a tree, afraid of the Beanstalk Giant would make a great group, all linked by a common emotion of fear. A cluster of teammates praying before the big game would make a great group, all linked by a common emotion of tense camaraderie. A cluster of children gathered around the Wells Fargo Wagon, waiting to get their instruments from the Music Man would make a great group, all linked by a common emotion of thrilled anticipation. Or the Von Trapp children arrayed in a group on Maria's bed during a thunderstorm would make a great group. You get the idea. Generally speaking, the chorus in a musical or operetta consists of people who are sharing an emotional link, as they are all singing the same lyrics. They would be well served to be staged in groups. Groups can consist of as few as two individuals, (in which case we could also call that relating) such as a husband and wife who are confronting an intruder in their home, or two drunkards who are staggering home from party. Generally speaking, if there are two or more people on the stage who share a common emotional link, it is better visual story telling if they are linked in a group. If their emotional link is broken, their group should break. If one character shifts emotional loyalty from one character to another, the groups should shift accordingly.

For the sake of the training, lets presume to be working with mostly large casts, such as the chorus of a musical or operetta. If you train them properly, and side coach them conscientiously, you can get a stage full of tight groupings in less than five seconds. That's right, in less than five seconds, simply by giving one side coaching command. Side-coach: *Groups in 5, 4, 3 ,2,1.* Or, *Tighten your groups*, or simply, *Group!*

Form Tight Groups

Tight groups are another very important element in the skill set of the facilitative director. I can't emphasize this enough. Whenever I am invited to do a master class with a local company, or whenever I start a rehearsal series with my own company, I train the cast in how to make tight groups. It is number two, directly after teaching them to take their own space. .

In addition to this being an extremely valuable skill for the actors, it is also a lot of fun. Whenever we do it we get lots of laughs, applause, and general good feelings. That's a nice way to start a rehearsal series.

Once you have taught your cast to form tight groups they can do it amazingly well in mere seconds. In otherwords, you can go from having a stage crowded with meandering elephants to having beautiful, dynamic, story-telling groupings in just seconds. And that doesn't mean they are running to assigned places. No, it means they can create brand new groups, with people they have not done any planning with, and create powerful groups in under five seconds. I kid you not. I do it all the time.

First, let's define what a tight group looks like. Here are eight parameters of a tight group. When I teach my casts these parameters, I teach them one at a time, cumulatively. That is, I teach all of the parameters in one workshop, beginning with one, then adding another, then another, until the actors are adept at applying all of them quickly and collaboratively.

The Eight Parameters of Tight Groups

1. Touch. Characters must touch one another to be a group. This is fundamental to groups, yet is a very difficult first step for many actors to overcome. Watch actors on stage, and unless they are specifically directed to touch one another, they may go the entire

show and never touch another human being, except for something perfunctory like a prescribed handshake. A tight group is one in which people are touching one another with their bodies, not just with their hands: arms around a waist, arms over a shoulder, leaning back to back, laying a head on one's lap, pulling each other's waist as in a tug of war, wrestling, hugging, clasping the same object, helping an injured person walk, clutching one another in fear, leaning in for a closer look, and so forth.

2. No Visual Air Space. A tight group has no visual air space between the members of the group. Generally that means that the group cannot be standing side by side, hip to hip. Instead, the tight group has higher people standing behind the shoulder of lower people. Getting behind or in front of one another is the best way to remove the visual air space.

3. Asymmetry. Unless there is a specific reason for the groups to appear formal, characters in the groups should array themselves in asymmetrical, or angular stances. Asymmetrical positions are most easily defined as angular, with each person in a different pose than anyone else. In an asymmetrical pose, the actor's body, if divided down the middle, would be different on each side.

In contrast, a symmetrical pose has the left side of the body mirrored by the right side. Symmetrical groups are characterized by people who stand at attention, or in formal rows. Save symmetrical poses for formal groups, such as a church choir, a military formation, a royal court, or a wedding. Formal groups are usually formal for the purpose of controlling or repressing emotion. An example of a formal group might be the Ascot scene from *My Fair Lady*. In that scene the aristocrats gather to watch a horse race, dressed in their formal wear. They sing a prissy gavotte about the excitement of the race, all the while behaving stiff, emotionally repressed, under well-mannered self-control. That stiff formality contrasts to the emotional outburst of Liza Doolittle who screams for her horse to "Move your bloomin' arse!" The emotional self-control is appropriately grouped with symmetry.

However, since most groups are linked by emotion, we avoid formality, we avoid symmetry. To be informal, be asymmetrical. To be emotionally connected, be asymmetrical. An example of an asymmetrical grouping situation might be the Jets in West Side story, or the mischievous monkeylike Wikersham Brothers in Seussical, or any of the groups in Seussical for that matter, or almost any choral group in almost any musical. If linked by a common emotion, they should be grouped asymmetrically.

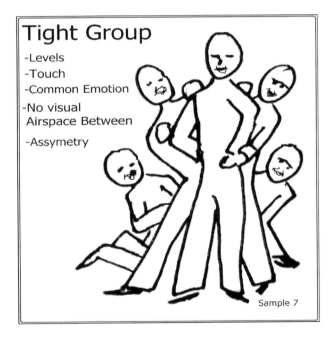

4. Levels: All the characters in a group should be at different levels. In fact, being more specific, each of the heads in the group should be at a different level. Sometimes that is natural. A family group, for example, often has the tallest father, the shorter mother, and two or three children at progressively lower levels. But a group of adults of relatively the same height requires that the characters select different levels. Some could be standing, others leaning, some sitting or kneeling, and another lying down. Regardless of how they get there, the heads should all be at different levels. The use of furnishings, such as benches, stools, stairs, trunks, and platforms helps actors create levels in groups.

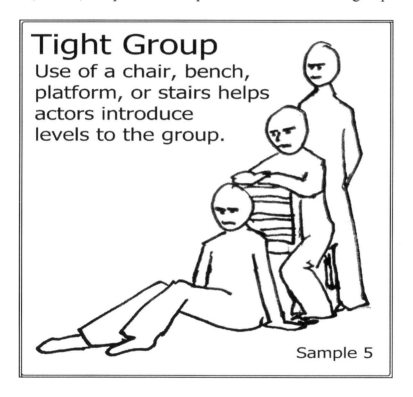

5. Heads toward the middle. A tight group has all the heads toward the middle of the group. Arms and legs can splay out toward the extremities of the group, but heads should be toward the center. Sometimes there are story telling tableaux where one head is not with the others, but that is dictated by story. An example of a group where one head is not toward the middle might be if four members of the group are accusing a fifth member of cheating. The fifth member might be leaning away from the others. If no story reason so dictates, put the heads toward the middle. Notice, for example, in the classic pose from the movie Charlie's Angels, the heads are toward the middle and the hands holding guns are out toward the sides.

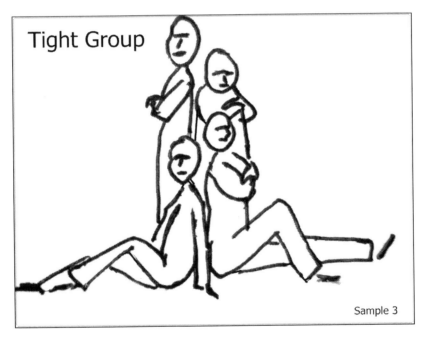

6. Common Emotion/ Story Telling. The group needs to decide on the emotional link that they share. Are they curious? Starving? Frightened? Cold? Mourning? Celebrating? Greeting? Stubborn? Exhausted? In love? Supporting a dying parent? Dreaming about going to America? Or, are they collectively telling a story through their grouping, as in a group of crap players rooting for snake eyes, or a group of boys peering over the walls into a girl's school, or thirsty sailors in a life raft scheming over one last canteen of water. Their group should tell the story or reveal the common emotion.

7. Balance the Stage. Once the ensemble is adept at forming groups with the first six parameters, they need to think and act as a full ensemble, and that is to balance the stage with groups. A balanced stage would have groups distributed on various planes of the stage, up stage and down, right and left, with roughly equivalent weight on each side of the stage. Weight is defined by the size of the group and the strength of position. A group of 7 people is as weighty as two groups of 3 and 4 respectively. But, of course, a group that is downstage or center stage is more weighty than one that is up stage or far to the right or left. In other words, a group of 3 who are down center can be well balanced by larger groups up stage and to the right and left.

8. Visual Air Space between Groups. Once the stage is balanced with tight groups, the groups need to be aware of the need to leave visual air space between the groups. For the stage to have room for movement, and visual elegance, there must be space between the groups. Otherwise, the groups run together, and become not groups, but a giant blob. No blobs allowed.

Advice: When working with children in groups, their attention to the grouping may wander, and before you know it your once-tight groups have dissolved into blobs. It is best to assign a responsible person, such as an older child or an adult to literally hold the group together. If that person, being the tallest, is in the rear, they can often put their arms around the wanderers, or, within their character, tug wanderers back into the fold.

Teaching the Ensemble to Form Groups.

Advice: This grouping workshop requires people to develop trust that they will not be doing embarrassing things. The best way to assure that is to (1) move one step at a time, and (2) stop to appreciate and ask for applause for actors who are accomplishing the goals. Take the time to find great examples, great groups, and ask them to freeze, while everyone else steps around front to see. These moments serve as models for others in knowing what it is you want, and it supports people in their creative use of their body.

This exercise takes about 20-30 minutes, although when you do it the first time, you might take longer. I usually combine it with other exercises to create a one to two hour training sequence that might include (1) stage position, (2) body position, (3) give and take, (4) crosses, counters, and pivots, and perhaps (5) approach avoidance, or status. It is important to review the grouping activity each rehearsal, to catch people up to speed who were absent, to remind actors that we expect groups all the time, and to make them comfortable with creating groups on a moment's notice. The review can take as little as a couple minutes. Once they are competent, your entire ensemble can form tight groups in less than five seconds. Imagine, going from a random, ugly blob of undirected chorus members standing around on stage wondering where to stand, to having a tight looking, balanced stage filled with dynamic groups of characters, in just five seconds. Yes, it is not only possible, it is simple. We do it all the time.

Step 1. Take Your Own Space. Direct the ensemble to *"Take your own space."* Taking your own space is an important yet simple organizing concept of free blocking. Actors should be taught that this command means they must select a spot on the stage floor that is distant enough from others so that they can move freely without bumping, a spot that is not on plane with others, such that they can see the director and audience without being obstructed by someone directly in front of them, and in spots that collectively fill the entire stage using whatever levels are available at the time. "Take your own space" is the proper way to begin warm-ups. In that case I add the word, "centered" to the command, in which case they know I want them to be relaxed, standing tall and symmetrical.

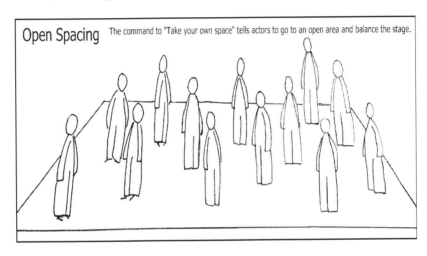

Open Spacing   The command to "Take your own space" tells actors to go to an open area and balance the stage.

"Take your own Space" is is also a very simple yet effective way of staging a large group. When actors take their own space they automatically create open spacing, or triangles. They automatically fill the stage, and if there are set pieces, platforms, or levels to use, they use them. If you have a choral finale where you want everyone to be seen, side coach them to move on a certain bar of music to take their own space, and watch how quickly your entire stage is filled with triangles of singers on various levels, balancing the stage. Notice too, that since they do this often, they can always go to a different spot, and it will work out, even if the personnel changes from rehearsal to rehearsal. They are not locked to a particular spot, rather they are expert at finding effective places to stand. The actors watch how the stage is filling, and they go to the empty spaces until the stage is full and balanced. Once actors are trained and comfortable with taking their own space it should take only five seconds or less before the entire stage is filled and balanced with no one blocking anyone else. To help people be comfortable with taking their own space, I might give the command several times, and ask them each time to go to a different place. Once they get there, and the stage is balanced, I will tell them, *"Good, now this next time when I say 'Take your own space' go to an entirely different space, watch where others go and balance the stage. When you are comfortable, relax and freeze there. You will have 5 seconds. Ready? Take your own space in 5, 4, 3, 2, 1, Freeze."* Repeat this a few times until people get comfortable with finding a space that meets all the parameters. Praise them.

Step 1 A. Take your own space with levels and character. This variation of the command to take your own space reminds actors that they should assume positions of variety, with assymetrical body positions, an various levels. Those down front should select a lower level than those in the back. You may end up with people sitting, kneeling, lying, reclining, bending, standing, either on the floor or up on some platform, steps, or furnishing.

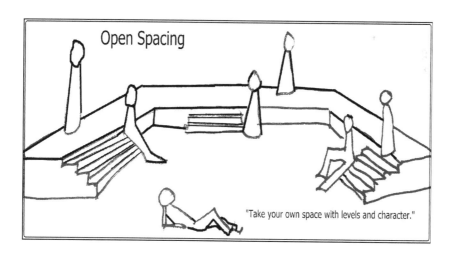
"Take your own space with levels and character."

Step 2. Reach Out and Touch Someone, Asymmetrically. You may need to review what we mean by "asymmetrical." Maybe have them move about and select angular, asymmetrical positions to freeze in. When they have that down, say: *When I say go, I want you to move out of your own space and touch someone else. When you do, I want you to be asymmetrical. You will have five seconds, then freeze while touching. Go, 5, 4, 3, 2, 1, Freeze.* This exercise usually results in a confused scramble, with people reaching out with their hands touching someone else on the shoulder, or foot, or top of the head, or hand. Sometimes the stage gets linked with long lines of people touching one another. It looks pretty bad, but don't say that! This is just the first step. Thank them. Let them laugh at the foolish ways they solved your challenge. Repeat it while asking them to touch someone else this time. Repeat it again a few more times, until people have begun to be comfortable touching someone other than their best friends. Then ask them to relax, not touching anyone, or to take their own space, while you explain the next step.

Step 3. Reach Out and Touch Someone Without Using Your Hands. Say: *This time, you will have five seconds to reach out and touch someone without using your hands. You can touch them with your shoulder, or butt, or back-to back, or legs, or any way you want, but no hands. Remember to be asymmetrical. OK? Go, 5, 4, 3, 2, 1, Freeze.* You will get some pretty creative ways of touching, and allow some laughter. Find the fun or creative ones, and call people's attention to the creative solutions to your challenge. Ask for applause for them. Repeat a couple more times, mixing with different people each time. By the end of step 3 people should be having fun mixing with each other, and getting comfortable touching.

Grouping Workshop

2. Reach Out and Touch Someone   3. Touch Without Using Your Hands

Step 4. Form a Group With 3 to 5 Members. Say: *This time we are going to form groups of people who are touching one another. You may use hands again if you want but try to be touching with other parts of your body as well. This time, I want you to condense together in the group that has anywhere from three to five members. No more than five. Ready? Go. 5, 4, 3, 2, 1, Freeze.* At this time, you will have several confused people who formed groups too large, looking for how to solve it. Help them solve it. Show them that an extra person can just walk out of a group and stand alone, and that other people will come join them until the group is 3 to 5 members. Standing alone waiting for others to join is leadership. Praise leaders. Repeat the exercise. Praise those who noticed the group was too large and who stepped out to start another group. Praise those who are frozen in interesting groups. Repeat a few more times, each time requiring that people mix up and form entirely new groups with new people. Don't worry about being critical if some group ends up too large, or too small. It's not a big deal. The 3-5 range is arbitrary, and flexible. Just praise those who kept within the parameters and move on. Once they are getting good at making groups of 3 to 5 members, ask them to relax and listen to the challenge for step 5.

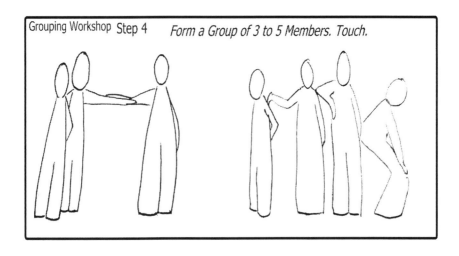

Step 5. Form a Group Where Each Member's Head is at a Different Level. Before doing this exercise, remind them of the different levels they can use, standing, bending, kneeling, sitting, lying propped up, lying down, or standing or sitting on someone or something. Sometimes I have them explore the levels, like this: Say: *Take your own space. Each time I clap my hands, go to a different asymmetrical position, at a different level and freeze there.* Then I clap my hands once, wait for the freeze, and repeat several times. Eventually people will begin to get very creative about their levels and asymmetrical positions. Furthermore, I often work with people of all age ranges and physiques, and this allows people with arthritis, bad knees, or a weight problem to make their own decision about what levels they are comfortable exploring. If I'm working with a group of kids, though, I make them all try every different level, because they love it. Stop after they get the idea without getting too wacky. Say: *Good work with levels. Now, This time, form a group of 3 to five members where each member's head is at a different level, touching each other, and asymmetrical. Go, 5, 4, 3, 2, 1 Freeze.* Note and

praise the unique positions and relationships people chose for their groups.

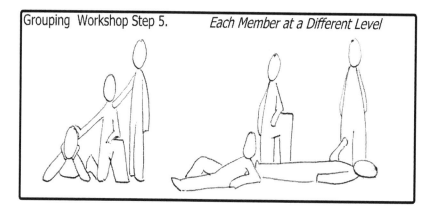

Step 6. Form Groups With All Heads Toward the Center.
Say: *This time, I want you to focus on forming groups with all heads toward the center. Remember, heads at different levels, asymmetrical body positions, touching other members of your group. Ready, Go, 5, 4, 3, 2, 1, Freeze.*

By the time you complete this exercise, you will be able to select some great looking groups to show off to the others. Point out the strong qualities of each group, heads at different levels. However, at this time the groups are not yet tight. Tightness is a function of step 7.

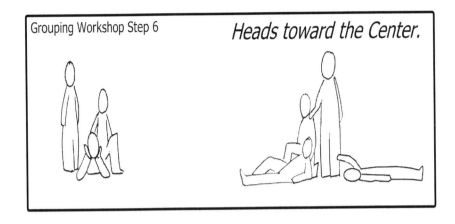

Step 7. Form a Group With No Visual Air Space Between Members. Say: *This time you will form a group of 3 to 5 members, with people touching each other, and with no visual air space between the members. Remember, you are an actor, and we want the audience to see everyone's faces, so make sure your group faces me, the audience.* DEMONSTRATE what you mean by no visual air space. Bring one of your most recent groups down front and position them so that some are in front of the others, not just side by side, so that there is no visual air space between them at the level of the torso. Say: *When I say go, make an entirely new group with new people, with 3 to 5 members, with no visual air space between members. Remember to use levels and asymmetry, and to touch one another. Ready? Go, 5, 4, 3, 2, 1, Freeze.* At this point you will have one or two groups that are looking very good, and some that are not there yet. This is where the command to freeze is important. Remind them to hold the freeze while you select some groups to use as models. Pick your best groups, tell them to hold the freeze, then tell all others to relax and come down front to see the groups. Lead applause for the model groups. Repeat this step only once or twice more, because it is important to add the next parameter.

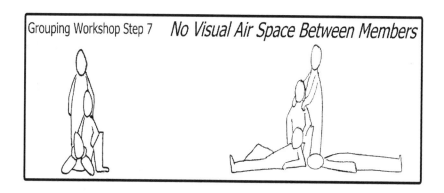

Now it is getting hard. That's OK. They have lots of trust in the process now, because you have done a lot to praise their work, and they have had moments of laughter, and moments of expertise that was recognized. No one has been picked on for not doing it well. Here is a good chance to ask people what problems they ran into. Maybe for the next time, let them use the same group of 3 to 5, so they have a few more moments to adjust their placement of heads. Maybe on a subsequent try they can keep the same group, but shuffle everyone's heads around. Different people up and different ones down. Advise them that no one is to plan, or give directions. Don't let someone take over and tell the others whose head should be highest, and where to put the others. This is not about planning, or someone being the decision-maker for others, this is about teaching every one of them to see the situation and make instantaneous adjustments themselves to create the tight grouping. When you get good looking groupings, ask them to freeze, and ask others to look at their group, and ask the others to point out what they did really well. Ask for applause for the model group. Use good groupings to illustrate how much better it looks, how much more unified the picture is when all the heads are toward the center.

Step 8. Form Groups with a Common Emotional Link. For actors, the play is about emotions, and reactions to emotional stimuli. It is not just about creating tight staging. The groupings we create must tell the story. They must be expressions of engaging emotions. They must be dramatic. Remind the actors that we use groups when characters have an emotional link, when they are feeling relatively the same feelings, feelings such as fear, sorrow, hope, thrill of victory, agony of defeat, passion, loss, mutual support, giggliness, raucousness, and so forth. Look to the lyrics of the songs and the tone of the play for the emotions that link the characters at any one time. Say: *When I say go, form a group that has a common emotion. I will tell you the emotion just before I say go. Remember, your group should have all the other parameters, touching, asymmetry, heads at different levels, heads toward the center, no visual air space between members, and 3 to 5 members. Your emotional link is 'fear.' Ready? Go, 5, 4, 3, 2, 1 Freeze.*

In selecting a common emotion for our tight groups, I always start with 'fear,' because it is easy for actors to group with that emotion, clasping one another, protecting the young, etc. (See Tight Group from Into the Woods) As before, select a few great groups for others to look at and praise. Encourage applause for the model groups. Repeat the exercise with other emotions, like "thrill of victory" or "dying of thirst" or "angry at the gods." Try to select some directly from your script or the lyrics of your songs. Select emotions you will actually be using, so that your actors see the link to how they will stage this particular show. I might pick lines from a song, like from Officer Krupke in *West Side Story*, there are marvelous lines, any of which could be used to form groups. "I am sick, I am sick...", (mock sick) or "Gee Officer Krupke, I'm down on my knees" (mock pleading) Or, from *The Music Man,* as the families on the street sing Iowa Stubborn they say things like, "And we're so goldurn stubborn we can stand touching noses for a week at a time and never see eye to eye" (Stubborn), or, "But we'll give you our shirt, and the backs to go with it, if your crop should happen to die," (generosity toward the downtrodden), or from *HMS Pinafore*, "Now this is most alarming, when she was young and charming, she practiced baby farming!" (alarmed). This is where the director helps the free blocking actors connect to their script through powerful storytelling images. I don't know how many times I have seen musicals, where the lyrics were sung by characters strung in a line across the stage with no organized emotional reaction to the words. Boring. Teach them to form groups, and teach them to link those groups through common emotions, and watch out for the creative power of the actors to shine through!

Sample 2

Step 9. Form Groups that Balance the Stage. For groups to balance the stage they should be (1) distributed about the stage, with (2) larger and taller groups in the upstage region, and smaller, lower groups downstage. There should be (3) visual air space between groups, creating a distinct visual separation of the groups. This visual air space also is movement space. Characters need to be able to move about the stage around and among the groups without being blocked or stepping on costumes. The groups should have a focus themselves, generally toward the audience. Upon occasion, such as when the groups are specifically gathered to watch a particular character they may shift their focus toward that character. So, when the Iowa Stubborn characters are gathered to watch Harold Hill sing "Ya Got Trouble in River City" they can focus on him. But when they are singing about being Iowans, make sure the groups are facing the audience. Say: *In this last exercise you will form groups, as tight as the ones you've just made, only this time you will balance* *the stage. That means you must distribute your groups to all the major areas of the stage. The largest and highest groups must be upstage. The smaller groups can be lower and downstage. There must be considerable air space between the groups for separation and for movement of other characters. The linking emotion is 'stubborn'. Ready? Go, 5, 4, 3, 2, 1, Freeze.* At the freeze, review the parameters of a well-balanced stage. Do you have a group up left? If not, ask one of the groups to move. Are your downstage groups smaller and lower? Is there visual air space and walking room between the groups? If not, ask some to move. Then ask them all to look around at the balance you have helped them create. Tell them that they are to do it themselves on the next tries. Encourage leaders to go to the empty areas of the stage to form the nucleus of a new group. Others will join them. Repeat, a couple times with a new emotional link.

Teach them to use any and all levels available to them. The set will have levels built into it, but they may not have the set for these earliest rehearsals. So, get out the stools, any available platforms, a step ladder, desks or beds, or whatever people can use to climb onto to create levels. Your groups must be adept at using levels, and at looking for objects that give them levels. If you train them well early, you will find them eager to use the levels provided by the set when it arrives. Otherwise, the levels on the set will not be used well enough and the set will appear as a burden that squeezes the stage into a smaller space. I recently saw a community theater show that had two great stair cases in different scenes, as well as other platforms, but, unless the actors were specifically blocked to use those stairs, all the action tended to avoid the stairs. That was too bad. The action was flat, all on the floor, and the stairs stood empty. In one scene there was a step ladder in the back, and no one got up on it, not once. People gathered in lines and couples along the floor in front of it, but no one used the level. Too bad.

Stage is balanced with a chorus of groups.
Even though there are 25 people on this small stage there is still plenty of room for a principal to move about freely.

Step 10. Assign Groups to Form on Specific Lyrics or Musical Notes. At this point, you are now ready to stage large group musical numbers using entirely free blocking techniques. You may assign actors to (a) form groups with a specified emotion, or (b) take their own space on specific lyrics or musical notes. Or, even more facilitative, you may ask the actors to look at the lyrics and brainstorm which lyrics would make great moments for forming groups or taking their own space. However you chose to make the selection, it is the lyric and the common emotion that you solidify early. The groupings and open spacings on the other hand, are still freely developed, and can change with every rehearsal. In fact, it is fun to change them every rehearsal. But, for the sake of strengthening your show, stick as closely as possible to the decisions about the lyrics and emotions that you made here.

Closure: This is a good time, if parents or friends or stagehands are in the audience, to have them describe how powerful the story telling images are from the groups. It helps reinforce for the actors that grouping beats straight lines every time. Another way is to divide the group into actors and audience, and have them perform a grouping exercise for each other. Always finish with applause and praise. Another way is to have them go back and try to repeat their very first step in the process, "Reach out and touch someone." Laugh together about how unsophisticated that was. But remind them that they, not the director, are the ones who created every one of those tight groups, and it is up to them to do it again, whenever called for, in five seconds or less.

Review this exercise in miniature each rehearsal. Within a short amount of time, people will jump right to the best groups they can make on the first try.

Villagers of Ploverleigh celebrate the betrothal of Alexis and Aline in the Gilbert and Sullivan Society of Maine's 2010 production of *The Sorcerer*

During rehearsal demand tight groups by side-coaching: *I need tight groups with the common emotion of _____ in 5, 4, 3, 2, 1.* Later, the side-coach will be even simpler: *Groups!*

After awhile you will notice that conscientious actors will automatically look for ways to link with other characters into groups. When they enter the stage space they will look for emotional allies, and will group with them. They will reach out and touch, they will pull themselves together, they will link emotionally, array themselves at various levels. Chorus members should especially look for opportunities to form groups without being asked.

I find it amazing, when actors who are steeped in the training of tight groupings interact with actors who are not as well trained. The "groupies" are touching, linking, seeking various levels, pulling heads toward the middle, etc., and the standard actors are feeling lost, disassociated, and resistant to the touching thing going on around them. The standard actors are out of touch with the groupies. The standard actors have no idea how to shape the stage picture. They are lost, confused, and resistant,and entirely dependent on the director. They need a good workshop on how to form tight groups. It is up to the director to make it happen for them.

Groups, Levels, and Asymmetry bring focus to The Master of the House from *Les Miserables*

Our exercises have been using random groupings. However, the actual rehearsals will use groupings of characters who have natural relationships or links. The tourists can link in one group, the Save-A-Soul Missionaries are in another group, while the gamblers link in still another. In "Iowa Stubborn" the groups are based on family units. In *West Side Story* the groups are by gang. In *HMS Pinafore* the groups are sailors, ladies, and officers. Remind actors to group according to common emotional links, and, of course, group according to relationships.

Manifest the Relationships

Relationships are invisible unless there is movement, positioning, and business (picturization) that reveal those relationships to the audience. Imagine two characters, a caring husband and wife, standing on stage, talking, deciding whether to send his mother to a nursing home. Their relationship is invisible to the audience, because there is no picturization, no manifestation of the relationship. But when she stands behind him as he sits at his computer, and she rubs his shoulders while they discuss the nursing home, the relationship is manifest. And any changes in that relationship can now be manifest. He may shrug off the shoulder rub. Or she may abruptly end it. Or she may ruffle his hair. Or he may lean his head back and savor the back rub. It is these actions, these manifestations of the relationship that tell the story visually. Side-coach: *Manifest the relationship with touch, business, and position.*

1. A relationship is how one character feels about another character at any one moment. There are strong bonds that keep some people allied throughout much of the play. But, usually the bonds of relationships are weaker than the pressure of the changing circumstances throughout the play. Someone's relationship to someone is usually changing in every scene. To help actors think about the dynamic changing of relationship, ask how their character feels about each of the other characters. When circumstances change, when surprising things are revealed, when suspicions grow, when insults are dropped, when schemers scheme, and when people are hurt, their relationships may change. As the director, watch for those moments in the play when new information is provided, when people have new feelings, and ask: *How do you feel about so-and-so now? Manifest it through your positioning, touch, and movement.*

2. Relationships are also the emotional, intellectual, and circumstantial links that bind characters together during stressful times. Characters in the chorus are often bonded by these feelings-in-common. When people are bound by these links, they should chose movements and positions that reveal those bonds. Bonds pull people together, or, at the least, to the same side of the stage. Educators have long noted that schools can be integrated successfully, yet at the free-form lunch tables, blacks tend to sit with blacks, and whites with whites. In a tavern, the aristocrats are likely to sit with other aristocrats, and peasants or hunters sit with their ilk. In times of external stress, families pull together. Side-coach: *Do you feel a bond with these people? Manifest the relationship with positioning, touch, and movement.*

3. Some characters are allies. They have a long term connection that is not easily breached, such as marriage, boss-and-secretary, military buddies, teammates, people of the same religion, best friends, or siblings. Allies usually have costumes with a common style. The gamblers dress differently from the Save-A-Soul Missionaries, carry themselves differently, and tend to cluster with their own kind. Visually, the composition tells us who see themselves as allies when they tend to cluster. Side-coach: *Manifest your relationship to your allies with positioning, touch, and movement.*

4. Some characters are rivals and have a long standing competition or enmity, which is not easily bridged. Rivals include war time enemies, athletic rivals, political polar opposites, and religious, ethnic or generational adversaries. Rivals are often staged with contrasting uniforms or costumes so that the rivalry is visually stated in color and style. Side-coach: *Manifest your rivalry with positioning, touch, and movement.*

Flow.

Remember, flow is the **series of dramatic movements** that **link tableaux.** It is movement; deliberate, graceful, emotionally laden movement, book-ended by tableaux. Generally, movement about the stage is one character at a time. There are of course many exceptions, and those exceptions provide variety, pace, and sometimes comedy. But, generally, one person moves at a time. The more people who move at once, the more important it is to bookend those large movements with tableaux. Generally, as a director, I like my beats to begin with a tableau, and rise in pace and intensity from there. The climax of the beat is another tableau.

Imagine this scene. I will describe it in a series of tableaus linked by movement. Stage left is a group of rescuers pulling a tattered girl from a crumbled bombed out building, working in a "rescue tableau." Stage right are clustered hopeful families behind a police line, in a tableau. Other groups such as news anchors, politicians, and curious observers are clustered about the stage, all in tableau. The movements that follow include (1) the emergence of the tattered child, (2) the recognition by the parents that it is their daughter. (3) Mom and Dad break through the police line and (4) run to their daughter, who in turn (5) hobbles toward them and stumbles to the ground, and the (6) family meet at center to hug and hold their rescued daughter. (7) The news anchors and videographers readjust their tableau to catch the moment. (8) The police try to hold back the surge of other hopeful families. (9) The villain, the bomber, slips away into the crowd. (10) The rescuers stop long enough to savor the "reunion tableau." In this example, a set of organized, story telling movements that have dynamic emotional elements link the opening "rescuing tableau" to the final "reunion tableau:" That is *flow*.

In a free-blocked show the actors invent the tableaux, and they create the movements that link the tableaux in response to their character's emotional urges. But, the larger the scene, the more responsibility the director bears in organizing that flow. Side-coach: *The scene opened with a tableau, and the tension is rising. Increase the pace of the movements, one character at a time, until we reach a climax, then hold that in another tableau.*

Teach the Ensemble to Flow

1. **Create groups** with a unifying emotion. Say: *Form groups with the unifying emotion of _____ . Go. 5, 4, 3, 2, 1, Freeze.*

2. **Characters change groups.** Groups can be dynamic, meaning they can change throughout the scene by people moving into and out of the groups. When a person leaves a group, the group readjusts. The person then walks to a different group, or to a solo spot on the stage. If it is to another group, that group absorbs the new person into a tight group. If it is to a solo spot, others may join that person to form a new group later. Say: *As I point to you, leave your group and move to either a solo spot on the stage, or to another group. The group must adjust to the loss of the person, and the new group must absorb the new person.* Snap your fingers each time you point to a new person. This moving from group to group can move rather quickly, as the groups practice adjusting to the loss of a character, and as groups absorb new persons.

3. **Characters Give or Take as they Change Groups.** As actors move to change groups, they become powerful, because their movement draws the focus. Therefore it is best for actors to change groups when they have a line. They are taking the stage. Occasionally it is important for actors to change groups when they are not to be the focus. In that case, they must move while giving focus to, or looking directly at, the speaker or while moving in a weak, upstage direction. Say: *As I point to you I will*

say "take" or "give". If I say "take", take the stage by moving to a solo spot. If I say give, move to another group while giving focus to (looking at) the person in a solo spot, or by making a weak movement to join a group further upstage. Point, snap your finger, and say, *Give* or *Take*.

DISCUSSION: This activity teaches actors to move from tableau to tableau, from group to group, and for groups to adjust when a person either joins or vacates their group. It is a great way to practice the concept of flow. During rehearsal, side-coach actors to group, to take, or to give.

Setting the Scene

Where am I coming from? What has just happened and how has that affected me emotionally? What is my objective? What am I struggling with? What am I afraid that I will encounter here? Setting the scene is a director's job, whether it is a free blocked show or not. I include it here to remind that setting the scene helps actors understand their emotions, and emotions motivate the blocking decisions that actors make. Without understanding the scene and how their character fits into that scene, all the free-blocking in the world is for naught. These questions should be answered collaboratively, by the actors, the partners in the scene, and the director. It is not a quiz show where there are only certain answers that are right. It is an exploration, a time to investigate, to posit ideas, and to explore those ideas intellectually.

Sketch from *Into the Woods*

Solving Common Staging Problems.

Fixing the Semi-Circles

The more people there are on the stage, the more likely they are to gravitate into a semi-circle, especially if they are acting on an open floor where it is easy for everyone to be standing. The principals may act in the center or at the keystone but gradually the extras form themselves into a semicircle around them. The semi circle is an amateurish stage picture. It blocks entrances and exits. It confines the principals to the center or keystone of the semi circle. It homogenizes the characters as equals. It doesn't portray relationships, and it has no depth. In a musical or opera it focuses the choral voices toward the wings. Avoid it. Here are some solutions.

Solution 1: First, point out to the actors that they have gradually formed themselves into a semi- circle, and that from here on out, semi-circles are outlawed on this stage. That provides them an intellectual motivation to watch out for semi-circles, and to solve the staging problem themselves, without the director having to intervene.

The quickest solution is for individual actors to change their stage position, body position, and stance. By that I mean they should move to a different plane than the actors around them, (try moving upstage if you are standing, or, if you are going to sit, kneel, or lie, you may move downstage) and select a body position that is weaker than the principals. And, generally speaking, that will force you to select the alert stance in order to maintain eye focus. If you are relating to another actor, take that actor with you as you move to a different plane. The director might side coach: *Stagger your line. Interrupt the semi circle by moving out of line.*

Solution 2. Another solution is for the director to call out either one of the two cardinal arrangements: (a) take your own space, or (2)form groups.

Solution 3. Another way to solve the semicircle problem is to stop the bad habit of staging scenes on an open floor. Get set pieces, furnishings, platforms and broad stairs into the set, and get actors up onto them, which should give them the opportunity to create levels, asymmetrical positions, and character revealing tableaux.

However, even in an open floor, actors should know that when you give the directive to take your own space or to form groups it includes the challenge to use lower levels in the down stage areas, and higher levels upstage. In otherwords, someone should find a motivation to sit, lean, kneel, lie, or get up on something and your staging will have depth and levels almost instantly.

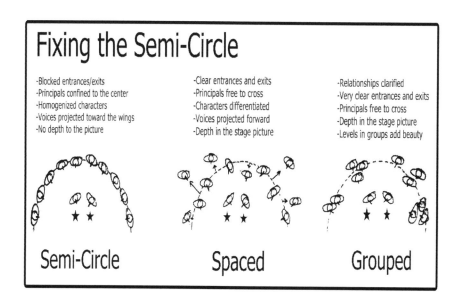

"Don't turn your back to the audience when you speak."

Invariably an amateur actor will at some time make a down stage cross while speaking to someone upstage, or, will speak to someone who is upstage of them, and will make the cardinal mistake of turning the head upstage during the line. Though it is easy for the director to sidecoach, "Don't turn your back to the audience when you speak," it helps if you have a quick solution to teach them.

Solution. Make the downstage cross as an away move. And do not turn to face the actor you're addressing until you have finished the line. Be careful, because amateurs will be tempted to turn near the end of their line to look at the addressee, finishing the line upstage. Don't let them do that. Remind them to finish the line in the face away position, then pivot to look, or glance over the shoulder, or, just remain facing away.

Dynamic Composition through Side-Coaching

Dynamic composition is stage positioning that tells the story, reveals relationships at that moment, projects the energy of the moment, and is balanced and attractive to look at while still giving focus to the principal characters and plot. To achieve dynamic composition, actors should be skilled in the strategies of free blocking, and should exercise their own decision making in response to side coaching instead of being assigned where to stand. Those assignments often deteriorate into unsightly lines, V's and semicircles, whereas actors choices often are more rich, flexible, and dynamic when they have the wisdom and responsibility to chose effective stage positions.

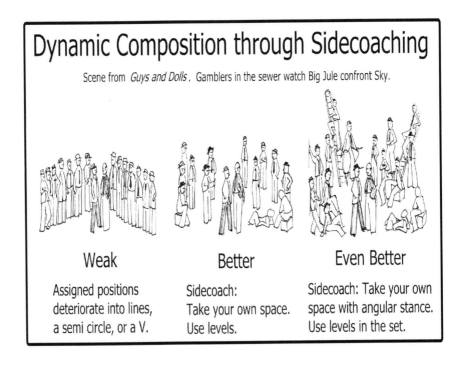

Workshop 4 -- GROUPING

Review Workshop 2 (3 min). Say: Take your own space in 3, 2, 1. Freeze. Pair up with hands on shoulders. Appoint hero and buddy. Do what I say, and repeat the name of the movement on "go" Take a sharing position, say "sharing Position" Go. Hero face away. Say "face away," Go. Both sharing, say "Sharing Position". Go, Buddy face away. Say "face away" Go. Both sharing, Go. Hero cross in front, say "cross in front". Go. Buddy cross to, say "cross to," Go. Hero pivot back, say "sharing position." Go. Buddy cross away stop facing away. say "cross away." Go. Hero, upstage cross to starting point, say "Upstage Cross." Go. Buddy upstage cross, say it. Go. Sharing position. Now improvise dialog with a movement on your line. Say whatever you want, but start with either "Will you" or, "Of Course" don't finish till each of you has done all of the movements in any order you feel.

Say: "Take Your Own space."

Teach. There are only three ways that characters can be arrayed on stage, one is open spacing which you can do in three seconds, the second is in lines, which we will not practice, because lines are for formal moments, and should only be done when the director or script call for it. Most of the time on stage we try NOT to be in lines. The third array is in groups. Today we will learn to make beautiful and expressive groupings. You will get so good at it that you will be able to make awesome full stage tableaux that express emotion and character in less than five seconds. You will then have the skill to place yourselves and move yourselves in ways that create focus and beauty on stage. The last skill we will learn in our next workshop, and that is how to connect movement, focus, and beautiful groupings to the script and the characters.

Lets learn how to make beautiful groupings. There are 8 parameters to beautiful tight groups. We will learn them one at a time, adding them together until we do all 8 parameters with every grouping.

Say: Go somewhere else on stage and take your own space, centered. I will give commands. Do not move until I say Go. I will count down from 5, and then you will freeze.

1.. **Touch**: Reach out and touch at least one other person. Go. 5, 4, 3, 2, 1, Freeze.

Good. Reach out and touch someone else. Go. 5, 4, 3, 2, 1 , Freeze.

This time touch someone entirely different. Go, 5, 4, 3, 2, 1. Freeze.

Good. This time touch more than one. Go, 5, 4, 3, 2, 1 Freeze.

Good. This time see how many people you can touch. After you freeze I will count who has the most. Go 5, 4, 3, 2, 1 Freeze.

(This may be funny, so enjoy it with them) Then Relax. Take your own space, centered.

2. **Touch with the Body.** Say: This time touch at least one other person without using your hands. I don't care if you touch heads, butts, elbows, hips, or whatever, just no hands. Go. 5, 4, 3, 2, 1 Freeze. (this will be fun, so it's OK to celebrate the creativity)

Good: This time touch at least two other people. No hands. Go. 5, 4, 3, 2, 1 Freeze.

Good. Relax, and take your own space.

Teach: In order to have a group onstage, people must be touching. If they are not touching, they are in open spacing. So, if the director calls for groups, always touch, either with your hands or body.

3. **Group of 3-5 people.** Groups can be any size from two to infinity, but for tight groups that look beautiful, we want 3 to five people. This time I want you to form a group of 3-5 people, touching with the hands or body. Go. 5, 4, 3, 2, 1, Freeze.

Some groups are too big. That means we need a leader to step out from a group and stand alone. Others will join that leader. Can a few leaders step out? Good.

Lets do that again. If a group is too big, I need some leaders to step out and stand alone, and others will join them.

Groups of 3-5 people. Go. 5, 4, 3, 2, 1 Freeze. Better. Lets mix it up each time. Go to a different part of the stage, group with entirely different people, in groups of 3-5. Go. 5, 4, 3, 2, 1, Freeze.

4. **Heads at different levels, visible to the audience.** Say: A tight group has all heads at different levels and visible to the audience. Form a new group of 3-5 people, all touching, with all heads at different levels. Go. 5, 4, 3, 2, 1 Freeze. Good. Now, with new people, form a tight group with all heads at different levels. Go. 5, 4, 3, 2, 1, Freeze.

5. **No Visual Airspace Between Bodies:** Demonstrate by taking a sample frozen group and sliding the people in behind one another to remove visual air space.
Say: Form a tight group, 3-5 people, all heads at different levels, with no visual air space between bodies. Go, 5, 4, 3, 2, 1 Freeze.

By now, you have some nice groups. Tell one or two of them to stay frozen, while the others break and come down front to look. Offer applause. Repeat. This time, let every group re adjust itself after the freeze, to tighten up. Do not allow anyone to boss the group, or to tell others where to go. It must be organic. Everyone is responsible to look at their group and to contribute, on the fly to making it work.

6. **Heads toward the center.** The legs and arms and props can splay out to the sides, but the heads must be toward the center. Think Charlies Angels, where their famous pose has one woman with her gun pointing left, one with the gun pointing right, and one with the gun pointing up. The bodies and heads are toward the center of the group. Form a new tight group with touching, with 3-5 people, heads at different levels, and all heads toward the center. Go. 5, 4, 3, 2, 1 Freeze. By now, there should be some really nice looking groups. Pick out a couple to hold their freeze, and have the others come down front to look. Applaud for them.

7. **Emotionally Linked:** Each group must be emotionally linked. This is how the groupings connect to the plot, to characters, and to the lyrics. This time, before you form the group I will tell you the emotion. With all new people, form a tight group of 3-5 people, with heads at different levels, no visual airspace between bodies, heads toward the center, and with the emotion of SCARED. Go. 5, 4, 3, 2, 1 Freeze. Awesome!

Again, show off some of the groups, and lead applause. Take pictures of all the groups.

Repeat, with the following emotions, and stop to show them off. If there are parents or techies, or other visitors in the house, have them offer applause too. . (a) investigating an ant hill, (b) angry at one member, (c) comforting, (d)celebrating, (e) worried, (f) looking into the future, (g) escaping, (h) listening to Mama read a bedtime story. etc.

8. **Balance the stage.** Teach: Balancing the stage means there must be groups scattered about the stage, up left, down left, up right, down right, and center, and so forth. The groups down front must be lower. No group should be directly behind any other group. The groups upstage should be higher, or up on something, and there must be visual air space between every group, so keep them separate.

Say: Form new groups, with 3-5 people, with heads at different levels visible to the audience, with heads toward the center, balancing the stage, with the emotional link of DYING OF THIRST. Go, 5, 4, 3, 2, 1, freeze. Great. Make any adjustments to assure that the stage is full, balanced, groups in front are lower, there is visual air space between groups. Take pictures of the groupings.

Repeat, with the emotional link of FREEZING COLD, then CELEBRATING, then SNEAKING, then RESCUING one of the members.

Tell the cast to thank each other by name, and mentioning something they did that you liked.

Chapter 10

More Ideas for Stage Movement

Meaningful Movements:

In addition to the fundamentals of crossing, countering, approach-avoidance, and give and take, there are other graceful movements that help to tell the story and to provide flow from one tableau to another. Here are several simple meaningful movements that the director can encourage through side-coaching. These are particularly helpful in auditions or the early stages of rehearsal. You will not have blocking and graceful flow unless there is movement.

Reach Out and Touch Someone.

A touch is a powerful visual and emotional connection. It also reveals the internal struggle: "Do I touch, or do I not touch?" It also gives the other character something to work off, something that reveals their own personal struggle: "How do I feel about this person touching me, and does that complicate things for me?"

Sidecoach: *Reach out and touch someone.*

Put the Struggler in the Middle.

When there are three (or more) characters on the stage, and they are in conflict (which is usually the case) the person who is struggling should position himself or herself between the others or at the apex of the triangle. That forces the character to look one way, then the other, or to move one way or the other as the alliances shift. This looking left and right is motivated by an attempt to either read their reactions or to speak convincingly, or to figure out what is going on. The facial expressions of the person in the middle become pointed to the audience. In contrast, if that same person were standing to the side, it would be difficult, even impossible to tell, from the audience perspective, which of the other two characters in front of him he is looking at. Put the person with the struggle in the middle, and it becomes very clear. When that person is done with the struggle, she should then motivate herself to move out of the middle, to move away, and give that middle position to someone else.

Struggles are common in plays, so this should happen often. Ask your actors to motivate a move to the apex of the triangle when their character is struggling with some discovery or some worry that involves two or more other characters on stage. When the struggle is resolved or clarified the character should move out of the apex, out of the middle, and leave that important spot for the next person who is struggling. Sidecoach: *You're struggling to understand what is going on. Move to the middle (apex).*

Here are some examples of strugglers who should be in the middle.

In *Guys and Dolls:* Arvide comes back to the mission after staying out all night trying to save souls. He finds granddaughter Sarah arriving home at 6 a.m. with Sky Masterson. He struggles to figure out what is going on. Have they been together all night?

Until he figures it out, he is best blocked in the middle. Once he figures it out, he can move out of the middle. Then, perhaps Sarah moves to the middle as she struggles to explain what she has been up to and as she struggles to understand what is happening in "the raid" as gamblers come running wildly out of her mission, chased by the police.

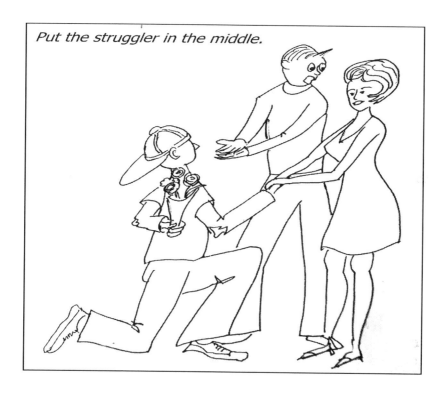

Put the struggler in the middle.

As a director, ask yourself, "Who is struggling to figure out what is going on?" Or, better yet, as a facilitative director ask the actors to tell you who is struggling. When they identify a struggle, encourage them to move to the middle, or the apex, until they have figured out the situation, and then to yield the apex to another character. It is another form of give and take.

Sidecoacch: *Who is struggling? Put the struggler in the middle.*

Lead with the Head

Graceful turns and movements are fluid, not stiff. They happen in overlapping sequences, with one part of the body moving first, and other parts of the body following. When there are changes in mood or motivation, it is graceful to lead with the head. For example, imagine your character has been crushed emotionally and is kneeling in distress, and then, in a change in mood, there is hope. Hope first lifts the head, followed by the shoulders and chest, and then the legs lift the body off the floor.

In contrast, if one is hopeful and then falls into despair, the head drops first, followed by the shoulders, followed by the chest, the torso, and the legs. (In this particular case, the despair might begin with a drop in the shoulders, as hope resides in the shoulders.) Furthermore, if there is a change in motivation, people need to move, and to lead that movement with the head. For example, when one is curious, turn toward the object of curiosity with the head, and then move toward it, leading with the head. Or, as another example, when one is ready to go somewhere, turn toward that direction leading with the head. The rest of the body will follow.

In a comedy, it is humorous to exaggerate leading with the head as it amplifies the change in mood, or it clarifies the depth of the motivation. Comic actor Jim Carey is famous for leading with the head, in exaggerated form. It is part of his schtick.

Lead with the Chest.

When you are falling in love with someone, move toward them gracefully while leading with the chest. The chest houses the heart. The chest lifts as breath is taken in. Desire resides in the chest, and like a magnet, the chest is pulled upward and toward the would-be lover. Again, in farce, leading with the chest can be exaggerated.

Lead with the Wrist

When a character is behaving in a graceful fashion (as in ballet, 19th century drama, Moliere and the high fashion of the French 17th Century) arm and hand movements are graceful when you lead with the wrist and let the fingers drift behind. When the wrist stops and pulls back slightly, the fingers continue their flow until they are fully extended. Leading with the wrist is appropriate when the hand flows in any direction, left or right, up or down. Ballet dancers know that the most graceful hand position is with the two center fingers held side by side and slightly curled. The outer two fingers are slightly separated and somewhat more straight.

Of course there are as many exceptions to leading with the head, the chest, and the wrist as there are reasons to do them. But, as fundamentals, it is best that the actor practice these graceful movements such that they are a part of the actor's movement repertoire.

Project Energy From Your Core Out Through Your Fingertips

Important gestures begin not with the hand, but with the heart, the impulse, the desire, the need. They begin at the core, the gut, the breath, the beating heart. Then they flow, like a slow moving current of power, from the core, through the shoulders, out the arms, through the wrist and hand to the finger tips. An important gesture, such as a reach, an appeal, a point, or the holding away of something terrible, has a tension that must begin at the core and end at the finger tips. In fact, imagine that it does not end, but rather continues to flow past the end of the fingers toward the other character, almost like an invisible force of will.

Back Away Then Turn to Run.

One of the most graceful movements to reveal an internal conflict is to back away then turn to run. Starting to move away, backwards, while still looking at the other person shows that your desire to leave has not yet overcome the need to stay. When you finally turn to run it is as though the conflict has taken a new turn, the desire to leave is momentarily stronger. Side-coach your actors to reveal their internal conflict about leaving by backing away first, then turning to run. When you finally turn to run, it is most graceful to lead with the head. In musicals, where grace of movement is reinforced by orchestral accents, it is particularly effective to employ this sequence. A musical actor may employ this sequence up to three times in one show. Used too often, it begins to be a predictable ploy. Used judiciously, it lends grace and visual impact to internal conflicts.

Stop Yourself from Running Away

As a fitting follow-up to the above movement, it is graceful and dramatic to stop running away, after as few as three to five steps. You must motivate yourself to stop. Some internal dialogue that may serve as a motivation to stop include these subtexts:

a. Wait, I can't leave without saying more.
b. I can't leave when you are calling to me. I am drawn to your words.
c. I can't leave, as I don't know where I am going.
d. I can't leave because my will to stay is greater than my will to leave.
e. Wait, I can't leave until I have gathered myself together.
f. I am not a coward. I can stay and face it.
g. I am so angry that I must stay until I make you angry too.
h. Please, don't let me go. Please ask me to stay.

Slow Reveal or Quick Reveal

Reveal an initiating reaction with a slow turn from back to front. An initiating reaction is one that begins a scene. It is the reaction to a new piece of interesting news. It starts the scene with slow, controlled movement that indicates increasing interest in what one just heard. This requires a set up, meaning that the person who is going to take the slow reaction must first assume a position that faces somewhat upstage, and away from the instigator. It's easy to motivate such a set up through the manipulation of a prop (put the coffee pot back on the stove, go look out the window, start to leave the room, hang up your hat, and so forth). A <u>slow</u> turn from back to front is for reactions that <u>start</u> a scene. For example, when Marion tells her mother, "Momma, a man has been following me all over town" it initiates the scene, and Momma is very interested, so she takes a slow reveal, as she says a long, drawn-out, curious, "Oh?"

Another example is the first line of Edna (played in drag by Harvey Fierstein) in the Broadway production of *Hairspray*. Edna, who takes in ironing, held a piece of laundry in front of her face until time for her first line. Then the laundry lowered, revealing Edna's plump and less-than-feminine face as Fierstein's distinctive scratchy bass voice uttered her first line to great applause.

Sidecoach: *Set up for a slow reveal by hiding your face, or turning back to the audience.*

In contrast, reveal a disturbing reaction with a quick turn from back to front. A quick turn is for a disturbing discoveries in a scene, a moment of rising tension. Again, the reveal from back to front must be preceded by a set-up. Get the reactor turned upstage and away from the instigator. When the instigator says the disturbing line, the reactor snaps around quickly, with great emotional energy.

Get the Feet Moving

When a character has a growing urgency to do something (and this happens a lot in a play) get that character moving his or her feet. Start to go, come back, start to go again. This movement gives vent to the internal struggle. It contrasts the urgency that this character feels to the other characters who may be standing still. Get the feet moving, whether it be in quick shuffle steps, long strides, nervous vibrations, pinched wiggles, or rocking back and forth. But get the feet moving. Actors often need to be side coached considerably to do this. Don't let them move their feet for a few seconds and then stop. No. The point is that the feet are externalizing an inner urge that is growing, and will continue to grow until the person does something explosive, like running off, or jumping out the window, or slamming the door, or grabbing a gun off the mantle and running to the window. You get the idea. Side-coach: *Get the feet moving to reveal the inner struggle.*

For comedy, two characters who have urgency, and whose feet are moving, might find themselves both running and stopping, in a confused and crazed delirium, running into each other, making a mess of things.

Freeze the Feet of the High Status Character

Freezing the feet is the opposite of "get the feet moving", and certainly doesn't seem to be a meaningful movement. But it is. By "freeze the feet" I mean you should not let the dominant character yield to the temptation to chase his adversary, or to back that adversary down, nose to nose. Dominant wife should not chase the husband. Dominant boss should not stalk after her shrinking salesman. Chief of Surgery should not charge after the nurse who dropped the instruments. The energy comes from the dominant character's struggle to keep herself from chasing, stalking, or charging. In otherwords, the dominant father feels like running after his naughty son and grabbing him by the collar and shaking him, but he DOESN'T LET HIMSELF DO IT. He struggles to control his emotions. He freezes his feet. The rest of his body may vibrate with the force of his internal struggle, but his feet remain frozen.

Frozen feet do several things for the high status or dominant character. First, it removes the confusion that comes if the lower status character fails to back away, or runs out of places to go. When we were kids we would play "chase the girls." The only problem was, what do you do once you catch the girl? We never knew the answer to that. Similarly, if the dominant person chases, at some point there either has to be a catch, or an escape. Since the chase cannot go on forever it's best not to begin the chase at all, to freeze the feet and let the struggle be internal. Second, frozen feet helps the dominant character maintain a frontal or strong body position. Chase someone across the stage and you are likely to end up in profile. Profile is not as strong as full front. Frozen feet can keep the dominant person in full front position, the strongest body position on stage. Furthermore, visually, frozen feet, or stillness, creates an air of formality, and formality contributes to an appearance of high status. In contrast, feet that are moving visually define a lower status.

But most of all, "Freeze the feet" is a sidecoach that helps remind someone who shuffles or rocks or has other meaningless or frivolous distracting movements to get solid, to get strong, to be somewhere.

Sidecoach: *Freeze the feet.*

N.B. I read this some years after I first wrote it, and I wonder, What in heck was I thinking! Of COURSE there are times when the dominant character chases someone else! All I can figure is that I must have been coaching a student actor who didn't understand how to carry him or herself with dominance, someone who was moving around too much. So I left it in the book so you could see that it's OK if you don't agree with me. Sometimes I don't agree with me! On the other hand, perhaps I was working with a very, very, very high status character, like the king, or the baron, or the haughty princess, in which case, not chasing is fully appropriate, as there are servants who will do that for them.

Run

Whenever there is urgency in the scene, side coach the character to run; to run on, to run off, or to try to run but not be able to go very far. Running is the ultimate expression of urgency. It is a full body movement that not only reveals emotion, it creates emotion. When amateur actors are floundering in less-than-full-body acting I encourage them run. They can't act with just their voice when they are running. They have to make decisions about how to use their body to run, to stop, to avoid furniture, sets, and other people. They have to lift their voices to match their physical energy. See "Short Run," Running forces people to gain control of their bodies, for stages are usually cluttered with people or set pieces. Learning to start, to run safely, and to stop are skills that must be practiced. Practice running often.

Sidecoach: *There is urgency. Run.*

Cross

Cross toward, cross away, cross in front, or cross upstage. Motivate that cross as approach or avoidance. Balance the stage with those crosses, which means look for the open or unused space, and go there. Collectively, the characters should use the entire stage and it is up to each individual character to motivate crosses to assure that the entire space gets used by someone.

Sidecoach: *This is getting too stagnant. Someone has to motivate a cross.*

Relate

Move to another character with whom you have an alliance at this moment. Move away from the character with whom you have a disagreement. Touch the character you relate to, if possible, with business that reinforces the nature of the relationship.

Sidecoach: *Relate.*

Encourage Movement.

Encouraging actors to move is a hugely important function of the collaborative director. This is not the same as telling them to move, nor of telling them where to move. They must make the decision where to move and why, but remember, they are busy with lots of things going on in their heads as they rehearse, not the least of which is remembering their lines.

Actors need the director to give them permission and encouragement to move. A fundamental responsibility of the collaborative director is to recognize when a character has an urge to move and encourage the actor to fully realize that movement. Encourage them to expand upon that urge by actually moving, or creating a physical gesture of significance worthy of a tableau.

Here's how it plays out in a rehearsal. (1) Assign characters to act a scene, or to improvise a scene with motivations similar to the scene they are about to do. (2) Then watch them, and when you see small movements or gestures, recognize and validate those gestures and small movements as an urge to move.

"I see that you lifted your hand briefly toward her face. That's great. You felt an urge to reach out, perhaps to touch. Say that line again and expand that gesture."

Sarah then repeats the line and this time reaches out and touches the face, then drops the hand back down.

"Great, Sarah," I say, "That touch gave Jason something to work off. His skin felt that touch, and his eyes responded, and his breath became a little shorter as his character sorted out the implication." But, I am not satisfied with a simple touch, because I know that I am after flow, which is graceful movements that link one tableau to the next. We can't have flow unless we have tableaux, and a touch is one of the prime opportunities for a tableau. So I continue, "Sarah, can you hold that touch in a tableau so that we can impress upon the audience the impact of the touch, and the impact of Jason's reaction to it. Hold that tableau as long as you can."

"Sure" she says, then she repeats the line, reaches out and touches, and holds the touch longer.

Of course the next line is Jason's, and he suddenly has additional motivation for movement of his own. His character may feel motivated to reach up and take her hand in his hand and turn to face her. He may be motivated to push her hand away. He may be motivated to close his eyes and savor the touch. These are the fundamental effects of collaborative staging. Movement expresses the internal feelings, and motivates reaction from the other characters.

In another example, I might notice Arya leaning forward, or shuffling her foot forward as she speaks. "Arya," I coach, "I notice that you moved your foot forward slightly. I see that your character had an urge to move, and I want you to do that line again, and follow that urge. Step forward; make a substantial cross."

In this case, Arya makes a cross that was motivated by her character's reaction to the text and subtext. The director might then sidecoach her to remember approach-avoidance or other forms of give and take as she makes her move.

Sidecoach Actors to Move

Probably the most common side-coaching I give is to encourage movement.

Sidecoach: *Move. Motivate yourself to move.*

Sidecoach: *Motivate avoidance by finding doubt, or worry, or other struggle.*

Sidecoach: *Use the full stage. Consider crossing away. Consider an upstage cross.*

Sidecoach: *I noticed you leaned forward, as though you wanted to move. Follow through and go somewhere. Move.*

Sidecoach: *Struggle with that. Its tough to say that. Let the struggle motivate you to move.*

Sidecoach: *What is your relationship to the other character at this moment? How can you regroup to make a visual picture of that changing relationship? Move somewhere that reveals your feelings now.*

Sidecoach: *I notice you took a small step. Can you make that more powerful by taking more and stronger steps? If you don't have room because you'll run into him, then cross to him, then storm away.*

Sidecoach: *Reach out and touch someone. Actually, its stronger if you don't just reach out, find a way to get closer.*

Sidecoach: *Balance the stage. You have been playing this scene down right. You haven't yet worked the upstage, or down left. Someone needs to swing to the other side with a cross away.*

Sidecoach: *Since you are addressing this to everyone, why not address parts of the line to different people. Use runs and poses, or short runs to cross back and forth from one person to the next. See how that raises your energy and urgency?*

Side-coaching movement is the most powerful contribution you can make to enliven the flow of the stage picture and to expose the subtext. After awhile, they catch on, and you will sidecoach movement less and less, as they learn to move of their own volition.

Trust the Process

There will come many times when your actors will ask, "What do you want me to do?" or, "Where should I go on this line?"

To the experienced director it is often easy to answer that question, and to fall back into the old routine of controlling the blocking process. It takes a great faith in the wisdom of actors to relinquish control and to allow the actors to shape the composition from a free form and unpredictable process. But emotions, relationships, status, objectives, internal struggles, and the subtextual messages from other characters should motivate the movements.

When they ask, "What do you want me to do? Where do you want me to go?" that's when the facilitative director asks simple clarifying questions:

Sidecoach: *What is your objective right now? What are you trying to accomplish right now? Is it going well? Are you worried? Struggle with that. And let any emotion that bubbles to the surface be your motivation to either approach or avoid.*

Sidecoach: *Do you need to be close, or do you need to put some distance between you as you struggle with this? If you need to move away, consider balancing the stage, and go to a part of the stage you haven't used recently. Then stop there, facing away. It will give the others something to react to.*

It is at such times that the collaborative director must trust the process, and avoid giving specific blocking directions. Rather, the best answer is to remind the actor to trust the process and to sidecoach. Remind your actors to motivate movement, craft the stage picture and tableau, and express subtext with these processes.

1. Allow the character's emotional flow to motivate movements that express the subtext.

2. Filter that emotion through the concepts of collaborative staging

3. Give and Take

4. Approach and Avoid

5. Form groups (in 5, 4, 3, 2, 1)

6. Touch others

7. Hold tableaux as long as the dialogue allows

8. Cross and Counter

9. Use Levels. Explore the vertical environment

10. Select asymmetry for the body position unless the situation is formal.

11. Express emotion through breathing, pace, and body position.

12. Look into the eyes of the other characters to read their response and to respond to their subtext more than to their text.

13. Discover and Reveal Internal Conflict – Struggle.

14. Balance the Stage

15. Take your own space.

When the actors concentrate on emotions, and let those emotions flow through the filter of the principles of collaborative staging, they no longer need to be told where to go on a particular line.

But it is the transition that is difficult for them. It is important for actors and directors to learn to trust the process together.

Remember, and I can't stress this enough. Free blocking is a rehearsal strategy. As the rehearsal progresses, the actors will gradually begin to repeat the same blocking. You do not need to push them into it. They will get there naturally. And by showtime the blocking will firm itself. It will be as solid as a rock by show time.

When they succeed, and even when they take baby steps toward success, recognize, affirm, and give thanks. You might just as well have fun. And so should they.

Chapter 11

Sample Scene

Stress Free Directing in Action using Free Blocking

This sample of directing uses the techniques from this book and the companion book in the Stress Free Theater series, *Coaching Pre-Broadway Actors.*

First is the bare script. Read it and imagine how you might block this scene in a traditional sense. Then imagine how you might stage it as facilitative director.

Remember, there are no right and wrong ways to do it, but there are more effective versus less effective ways.

Second is the script of the rehearsal of that same scene. I hope this example inspires you to be more effective.

From *The Pirates of Penzance* by W.S. Gilbert.

Background. Frederick, a pirate, turned 21 and aged out of his mandatory apprenticeship so he announced his plans to leave the pirate life, since it doesn't seem to pay, because the pirates are too tender-hearted. Whenever they capture a ship, all the sailors claim to be orphans, and the pirates, who are orphans themselves, let them go.

Frederick then stumbled upon a beach party of beautiful maidens. Since he had never seen a young woman before, Frederick promptly fell in love with Mabel. She fell for him, too.

But then, the rest of the Pirates of Penzance arrived and lustily decided to carry the maidens off.

Just in the nick of time the maidens' father came along. He's an old fool of a Major-General who introduced himself by telling them how he was such a super student, learning all about the history of warfare, mathematics, biology, and so forth, that he became the "Very Model of a Modern Major General." We pick up the dialog just as he finishes that song.

On stage are several Pirates and several Daughters. The stage is full of people.

General. And now that I've introduced myself, I should like to have some idea of what's going on.

Kate. Oh, Papa – we –

Samuel. Permit me, I'll explain in two words: we propose to marry your daughters.

General. Dear me!

Girls. Against our wills, Papa – against our wills!

General. Oh, but you mustn't do that! May I ask – this is a picturesque uniform, but I'm not familiar with it. What are you?

King. We are all single gentlemen.

General. Yes, I gathered that – Anything else?

King. No, nothing else.

Edith. Papa, don't believe them; they are pirates – the famous Pirates of Penzance!

General. The Pirates of Penzance! I have often heard of them.

Mabel. All except this gentleman – (indicating FREDERIC) – who was a pirate once, but who is out of his indentures to day, and who means to lead a blameless life evermore

General. But wait a bit. I object to pirates as sons-in-law.

King. We object to Major-Generals as fathers-in-law. But we waive that point. We do not press it. We look over it.

General. (aside) Hah! an idea! (aloud) And do you mean to say that you would deliberately rob me of these, the sole remaining props of my old age, and leave me to go through the remainder of my life unfriended, unprotected, and alone?

King. Well, yes, that's the idea.

General. Tell me, have you ever known what it is to be an orphan?

Pirates. (disgusted) Oh, dash it all!

King. Here we are again!

General. I ask you, have you ever known what it is to be an orphan?

King. Often!

General. Yes, orphan. Have you ever known what it is to be one?

King. I say, often.

Pirates. (disgusted) Often, often, often. (Turning away)

General. I don't think we quite understand one another. I ask you, have you ever known what it is to be an orphan, and you say "orphan". As I understand you, you are merely repeating the word "orphan" to show that you understand me.

King. I didn't repeat the word often.

General. Pardon me, you did indeed.

King. I only repeated it once.

General. True, but you repeated it.

King. But not often.

General. Stop! I think I see where we are getting confused. When you said "orphan", did you mean "orphan" – a person who has lost his parents, or "often", frequently?

King. Ah! I beg pardon – I see what you mean – frequently.

General. Ah! you said "often", frequently.

King. No, only once.

General. (irritated) Exactly – you said "often", frequently, only once.

DISCUSSION: In most productions the Pirates and Girls, which I will refer to as Daughters, have been standing around doing small dance steps and singing responses to the Major General's bragging patter song. The dialog is usually focused entirely on the Major General and the King, in the center of the stage, usually sharing, with a few crosses to mix up the action. But we will apply the principles of free blocking and capture the ideas of the ingenious cast and as a result we will make some interesting and more effective staging decisions.

GENERAL: And now that I've introduced myself, I should like to have some idea of what's going on.

DIRECTOR: Great. So lets make sure there's lots going on, so that the Major General is motivated to say that. What could be happening?

SAMUEL (a Pirate): I could have one of the daughters on my shoulder, heading off to the hills.

DIRECTOR: Great, grab someone and lift her. In fact, since Kate and you have lines coming up, why don't you lift her.

Samuel lifts Kate on his shoulder and runs off stage.

DIRECTOR: Great. But once you run off stage, you're gone, and we need you here. So the solution is to do a short run where you start to run, but motivate yourself to stop. What motivation could you have to stop? Everyone, help think of motivations to stop.

DAUGHTER 1. Maybe he sees another girl he wants more.

DAUGHTER 2. Maybe he doesn't know where to take her to be alone.

PIRATE 1. Maybe he is waiting for his friends, so they can go together.

PIRATE 2. Maybe he's afraid. His buddies coaxed him into this and he's a bit ashamed of himself.

DIRECTOR: Good, does that give you some ideas you can use to do a short run with a motivated stop? Pick something that works for you. OK pirates and daughters, what are the rest of you doing?

PIRATE 2. Me, too! (He grabs a daughter who kicks and screams!)

PIRATE 3. Me, too! (He grabs a daughter, and off they start, with a motivated stop)

PIRATE 4. Me, too! (He tries to grab a daughter, and she runs away, screaming. He chases her around the stage. Lots of screaming.

DAUGHTER 1: I'd like to flirt with someone more gently.

DIRECTOR: Great, pick someone and pull him to the corner and start flirting. What else could be happening. Lets have variety?

MABEL: I already have Frederick, so we aren't into chasing. More like making out.

DIRECTOR: Try it. There's a rock or beach chair down right you could use. The rest of you let's do it, and let your character decide how far you'll go. You are Victorian ladies, remember.

Mabel and Frederick go to a corner and recline amorously.

DAUGHTER 2: I've been playing the character of the older sister, kind of protecting my sisters. I think I would be confronting a pirate, or protecting one of my younger sisters, or maybe trying to protect all of them. I'm feeling pretty tough.

DIRECTOR. Try that. Anyone want to be protected? Any pirates want to try to get past the protective sister?

Eventually each of the pirates and daughters have selected some activity. There is lots of laughter from the cast, and lots of noise, ad libs, and some foolishness.

DIRECTOR: This is a lot of fun. Chaotic, but fun. So lets bring some order to these ideas. Everyone take your own space, as you might find yourself at the end of the Major General's song. It doesn't matter where, as we will organize that later.

Actors take their own space, filling and balancing the stage with a mixture of pirates and daughters. I'm going to give you only about 3 to 5 seconds to start to do all these things. The cue will be Major General's line, "And Now that I've introduced myself." At that point, take off, and do your thing. But stop when the Major General demands to know what's going on. You must GIVE for his line. Major General, your line... but wait five seconds before you say the second half of the line.

GENERAL: And now that I've introduced myself.... (chaos erupts, with ladies being carried off, flirtation, chasing, etc.) I should like to have some idea WHAT'S GOING ON!!!!

DIRECTOR: Great! You sure were motivated to ask what's going on! How do you feel?

GENERAL: I'm very upset. These are my daughters, and they appear to be having altogether too much fun (looking at Mabel and Frederick) and they may be in danger.

DIRECTOR: What else do you feel?

GENERAL: Mad.

DIRECTOR: At whom?

GENERAL: At my daughters. At these strange men. At myself for not being able to stop it or control it.

DIRECTOR: Let those feelings, whichever ones pop to the surface at the time, motivate you to move somewhere, to do something. What could you do?

GENERAL: I might try to stop one of the pirates from hauling off a daughter.

DIRECTOR: What else? Anyone with ideas?

KING: He might try to poke people away from his daughters with his umbrella.

DIRECTOR: Good. What else?

Daughter 2. He might run and hide behind me, being afraid and intimidated by all the energy.

GENERAL. I like that. Instead of being in control, I seek refuge behind my own daughter who is fending off the pirates. That's funny.

DIRECTOR: Those are some great choices. See how any of those movements might give us insight into the complexity of your character. Let's do it again, and do any of those that you feel in the moment as you see the chaos erupt.

Remember to freeze, or give, when Major General demands to know what's going on. The next line is by Kate, who is on someone's shoulder, so give and let her say her line without interruption.

OK, take your own space, end of song. Major General, your line.

GENERAL: And now that I've introduced myself...(Chaos erupts again with lots of chasing and flirting. Major General chases after Kate who is on Samuel's shoulder, then hides behind his tough daughter) I should like to have some idea...(He runs around desperately) WHAT'S GOING ON!!!. (This chaos freezes in place)

KATE: (from Samuel's shoulder) Oh, Papa – we – Can Samuel swing me so I'm facing downstage? (Samuel does it)

SAMUEL: (Spinning around to face the General, Kate still on his shoulder) Permit me, I'll explain in two words: we propose to marry your daughters. (grinning broadly)

DISCUSSION: At this point it is common that someone, either the Major General or Samuel counts the "two words" on his fingers, counting up to six, and mugging the quizzical look of being wrong in the count, but, gosh, what is happening in this scene now is too exciting to stop everything to push that joke. Do it if you want, but don't let it stop the energy.)

GENERAL: Dear me!

DAUGHTERS: Against our wills, Papa – against our wills! (The daughters all kick and struggle.)

DIRECTOR: Is it really against your will? I see flirtation, I see smiles of joy and thrill. I think that at least some of you are excited as well as worried.

KATE: The words say it's against our will, so we should all be fighting. We should not be excited.

DIRECTOR: The fascinating thing about dialog is that the authors has composed the words you use, but not the feelings you have. Humans often say the opposite of what they feel. Ask a distraught person how they feel and they often say, "I'm fine" as they collapse in tears. Or ask a nervous bridegroom how he feels as he awaits the ceremony, pacing, sweating, constantly checking to see if the best man has the ring, and he'll say, "I'm fine," when he is just trying to convince himself and others that he is fine, when he really is at his nervous worst. So it is with these words, "Against our will." Different characters may have different feelings as they say that. So, again, I ask, is it really against your will.

KATE. For me it is.

DAUGHTER 1: For me, I'm thrilled, but terribly worried.

MABEL: I just mumble it to be supportive of my sisters, because I am falling in love with this guy.

DAUGHTER 2. For me it's fun, as long as Papa can protect us.

DIRECTOR: Good. Each of you bring a different meaning to that phrase, and let your lusty pirate know your subtext. Pirate, you read it clearly, and respond to how she says it, OK? Lets see where that takes us. Take it from "Against our will..."

DAUGHTERS: Against our Will, Papa, Against our will!

GENERAL: Oh, but you mustn't do that!

DIRECTOR: Mustn't do what?

GENERAL: Marry my daughters.

DIRECTOR: True, but what's happening around you?

GENERAL: Crazy things. My god, Daughter 3 is lucky she still has her clothes on!

DIRECTOR: Great, let one of those crazy things motivate that line, and some serious movement to go with it.

GENERAL: Oh, (He runs to his flirty daughter and pulls her away from a Pirate) but you mustn't DOOOOO that! (There is lots of laughter from the cast because it was so funny.)

DIRECTOR: Good. That was really funny. But before we decide to keep it. Lets try that line with some other pairs of Daughter/Pirates, and see what happens.

GENERAL: OK: Oh, (He chases a daughter on the shoulder of a pirate. This time the pirate runs away, and around the stage and General chases them) but you mustn't DOOOO that! (Lots more laughter form the cast)

DIRECTOR: Very funny. But that could go on forever. How do we end it.

KING. He gives his next line to me. Maybe I could stop him so he's facing me.

DIRECTOR. Great. Try it again. This time General, since we're still exploring, try going to another pirate-daughter pair that is bothering you. Everybody, try being as outrageous as you can so he will come to you. Let's see what happens. And, whatever happens, King, you stop him. Remember, when King stops him, all freeze, so you give. They have the lines, not you.

GENERAL. OK. (At this point the chorus are over the top flirtatious, or screaming, or kicking, or making out.) Oh, but you mustn't DOOOO...OOOO...OOOO THAAAAAT! (General runs from one group to another, overwhelmed by all the things going on, and finally, after being held back by the King grabbing his coat, he collapses, center stage, almost sobbing in his frustration.)

DIRECTOR. Awesome. What fun! General, I loved how you tried to get to all of them, and the King catching you, and then you collapsed. But I love tableau, and touching. Instead of falling to the floor, can you collapse into the arms of the King, hang onto him for dear life, as if you would collapse to the floor otherwise?

GENERAL. (collapsing into the King and leaning so hard into him that he looks like a ramp leading up to the King's chest. He slowly begins to compose himself, as he touches, smells, and fiddles with the Kings costume.) May I ask – this is a picturesque uniform, but I'm not familiar with it. What are you? (General straightens up and looks at the King.)

DISCUSSION: As this dialog continues it is commonly staged that the General and the King are in a sharing position, two big wigs in their own different worlds, going wit against wit, bull against bull, letting the dialog carry the plot along. All well and good, and certainly acceptable. But, as a free blocking director I look for tableaux rather than sharing position. A tableaux is dynamic, and tells the story and relationships.

DIRECTOR: Oh I loved the leaning in. In fact, can you hold that tableau as long as the dialog allows. In fact, King, when you speak can you back away a small step until General is really leaning quite far. Steady him with your upstage hand so it doesn't show. Great, that looks so funny! General, you can use that position to try to catch your breath. Continue.

KING: We are all single gentlemen.

GENERAL: (Breathing in gasps) Yes, I gathered that – Anything else?

KING: (Steps back a bit) No, nothing else. (General is leaning very far)

EDITH: Papa, don't believe them; they are pirates – the famous Pirates of Penzance!

GENERAL: (He stands straight) The Pirates of Penzance! (He turns his head away) I have often heard of them.

MABEL: All except this gentleman – (indicating FREDERIC) – who was a pirate once, but who is out of his indentures today, and who means to lead a blameless life evermore.

DIRECTOR: Great. General, when you discovered that they are pirates you stood straight. Go further with that. Use that same motivation to motivate a cross away. Better yet, since Mabel has the next line, and since she has been amorously intent on Frederick, why don't you head toward her, it might interrupt her tete-a-tete and motivate her. Take the line again.

GENERAL: The Pirates of Penzance! (He shivers as he scurries away from the King in the direction of Mabel and Frederick.

DIRECTOR. See how that cross brought out more of your emotions?

GENERAL: I have often heard of them. (He looks at Frederick with scorn.)

MABEL: (Speaking defensively but still entwined with Frederick) All except this gentleman -(indicating Frederick by stroking his hair) who...

DIRECTOR: Good, and I liked Mabel being so loving toward Frederick, but, lets go back to General. It was awesome when you gave that scowl to Frederick, but, he didn't see it, and neither did Mabel. Can you do something that he will notice, so it gives them motivation? It doesn't matter what, as long as you interfere with the lovers. Give them something physical to work off. What do you feel like doing?

GENERAL. I feel like pulling him off her. Yanking those long locks of curly hair. I feel like poking him with my umbrella. I feel like grabbing Mabel by the hand and pulling her away. I feel like a failure. I'm in real trouble now, because these are real, honest to goodness pirates. They are not schoolboys. He could take a knife to me any minute.

DIRECTOR: Let any of those feelings rise to the surface and do what you feel is right in the moment. Take it from "The Pirates of Penzance."

GENERAL: The Pirates of Penzance! (Shuffles toward Mabel, more scared than before, looking around at all the Pirates, spinning as he does it, and ending up looking at Frederick.) I have often heard of them. (He kicks Frederick's foot. Then instant regrets it, as he might be in greater trouble. Frederick startles, and looks up angrily. Mabel jumps up to protect him.)

MABEL: All except this gentleman --(indicating Frederick, and putting her hand out toward him) who was a pirate once, but who is out of his indentures today, (Frederick takes her hand and gently pulls her back down to him) and who means to live (she smiles warmly at Frederick) a blameless life evermore.

DIRECTOR: Mabel, nice choice to allow Frederick to pull you back. General, how do you feel now, as you see Mabel cuddle up with Frederick again?

GENERAL: I'm beside myself with beffudlement. I'm overwhelmed. I'm not sure what to do. I wish I could call my army and let my soldiers and their officers come to the rescue of my daughters.

DIRECTOR: Lots of powerful emotions. Let powerful emotions drive a powerful move. Approach or Avoid but go with power.

GENERAL: (Strutting across stage, toward no one in particular) But wait a bit. I object to pirates as sons-in-law. (He stops DL facing away.)

KING: (Standing still, off C) We object to Major-Generals as fathers-in-law. But we waive that point. We do not press it. We look over it.

DIRECTOR. Give and Take. General give. King, take the stage. Do that line again.

KING: (Stepping to Center) We object to Major Generals as fathers in law. (General pivots to face him from DL) but we waive that point...

DIRECTOR: Good to give and take, each of you. King, is this approach or avoid for you.

KING: I'm annoyed by the little bumbler. I like intimidating him. It's approach.

DIRECTOR: Pick up where you left off.

KING: (stepping toward General) We waive that point.

(Stepping again) We do not press it. (General shrinks backwards) We look over it. (He hovers over a shrinking General)

DISCUSSION: The historic staging of this moment has a tall King towering over a shorter General, and looking over his head. Of course that's not an easy sight gag if your General is taller than your King.

Historic Photo. The Pirate King -Darrell Fancourt- looks over having a Major-General -Martyn Green- as his father-in-law.

DIRECTOR: Excellent intimidation. General, you responded to his hulking presence by shrinking. Extend that movement, Do it even bigger. Can you shrink even more?

GENERAL: (shrinking till he is almost squatting in fearful intimidation) Hah! an idea!

DIRECTOR: Take the stage.

GENERAL: (Shrinking, turning toward the audience) Hah! I have an idea. (standing and facing the King, somewhat upstage) And do you mean to say...

DIRECTOR: Give and take. General you are facing somewhat upstage.

GENERAL: That's because the King is upstage of me. Can he move down to be even with me?

KING: I can do that. (he steps down, sharing with General)

DIRECTOR: Pick up from "And do you mean to say..."

GENERAL: (Standing still) And do you mean to say that you

would deliberately rob me of these, the sole remaining props of my old age, and ...

DIRECTOR: General, aren't you being manipulative here? Since this is your plan, your ruse, why don't you behave a bit over dramatic, like you're launching into a melodramatic monologue. Your character attends theater. Try sweeping about the stage like a Victorian actress you admire.

GENERAL: Absolutely, love it. (Lifts his wrist to his forehead, and sweeps across the stage dramatically, adding fake sniffles and tears, quivering his voice, to much laughter from the cast) And do you mean to say that you would deliberately rob me of these, the sole remaining props of my old age, and leave me to go through the remainder of my life unfriended,(fake sob) unprotected, (fake sob) and alone? (deep sigh)

KING: (King, who had turned, following General through his dramatic display, now takes the stage, still center, by pivoting to FF.) Well, yes, that was the idea.

GENERAL: (Dancing on tip-toe back to King, and leaning on his shoulder, appealing) Tell me, have you ever known what it is to be an (pause) orphan?

PIRATES: (disgusted) Oh, dash it all!

DIRECTOR: OK, Pirates and daughters, your turn. I know this has been a long rehearsal and you pirates long ago set your lady down on the floor. but, since this is such key moment for you. We need you to be in full character when you say "Oh dash it all." What could you do at that moment.

PIRATE 1. We could collapse. Drop our lady.

DIRECTOR: Good, but set her down gently. No injuries, please. Just ACT like you're dropping her.

PIRATE 2. We could drop our head in our hands. He demonstrates.

DIRECTOR: Relate when you do that.

PIRATES 1 and 2 stumble toward each other and hang onto each other, comforting their disappointment.

DIRECTOR: What else?

PIRATE 3. (demonstrates, collapsing to the floor)

DIRECTOR: Who can be even more demonstrative than Pirate 3?

PIRATE 4. (collapses to the floor, kicks and screams like in a tantrum --lots of laughter from the others.

DIRECTOR: OK we have some options for the pirates. But daughters, what would you feel and do when pirates drop you and start acting so out of character, at least they no longer appear so masculine.

DAUGHTER 1. I'm relieved. I was scared. I would run to someone, maybe Papa, maybe to another sister.

DAUGHTER 2. We might run and hide. Peeking out from behind something.

DIRECTOR: Hide behind what?

DAUGHTER 3: The treasure trunk.

DAUGHTER 4: Papa's umbrella. (She demonstrates. Lots of laughter from the cast. Then she opens the umbrella and others run to hide behind it.)

DIRECTOR: We've been in an active tableau of girls being carted off. Now the tableau changes abruptly. Whatever your reaction, pirates and daughters, remember to relate, to form tight groups, and to balance, or fill the entire stage. Go somewhere that balances the stage as you reveal your emotions. Also, get into a position that you can freeze in for the duration of the "orphan-often" dialog that's coming up. So, no matter where you go, don't be center.

DIRECTOR: Let's try it a few times, trying something different each time, until you find things you like and that form a new and dynamic tableau. Return to your former tableau, being carted off or whatever. Good. Now take it from General's line, "Have you ever known..."

GENERAL: Tell me, have you ever known what it is to be an orphan?

PIRATES: (disgusted --dropping their daughters and collapsing into tantrums, disgusted groups, and pulling out their hair and pounding their hats on their knee. Daughters scurry in scattering movement, and cluster, comforting one another.

DIRECTOR: OK Freeze. Great. Tighten those groups! Look around, and see if the stage is balanced. (They move and readjust.) Good. Let's do that again, go somewhere else, form a different group, take a different reaction, but no matter what, focus on balancing the stage. You're making a tableau that must tell the story and hold for another minute. You will have five seconds for your reaction, then freeze. Back to your other tableau. Ready. General, your line.

GENERAL: Tell me, have you ever known what it is to be an orphan?

PIRATES: Oh, Dash it all. (They set down their lady, hunker in groups of disgust and dismay, collapse in tantrums, and melt into weak ineffectual men. The daughters each react differently, some disappointed, some relieved, and they form groups and relate, collectively filling the stage.

DIRECTOR: Great. And if there is someone here at the next rehearsal who was not here tonight, they can find their own reaction, go where they want, and form groups or take dynamic tableau positions that tell the story. If you go someplace else next time, remember to balance the stage.

Now, King, what is your reaction?

KING: I'm disgusted. I've heard this orphan excuse before, and I always fall for it.

DIRECTOR: Why do you always fall for it? Frederick just told you that all the merchant sailors always claim to be orphans, and you let them go.

KING: I thought about that when he told me. Maybe this time I'm even more annoyed with myself. I'm struggling with whether to be sympathetic toward the orphans or to stand up against the orphan lie, which everyone seems to be using on us.

DIRECTOR: Good. Struggle with that. You can be mad at yourself.

KING: (Rolling his eyes) Here we are again!

DIRECTOR: Good. Can you give me more of that struggle?

KING: (rolling his eyes, yanking off his hat and pounding it on his knee.) Here we are again! (General looks at him with incredulity)

DIRECTOR: Great. When you did that, the General had much more to work with. Can you do it again, and even give me more of that struggle, that anger at yourself. More, more, more. Angry!

KING: (rolling his eyes, grabbing his hat, pounding it on his knee, pounding the hat on the ground, and sitting on the ground pounding his hat --lots of laughter from the cast) Here we are again!!! (slamming the hat back on his head, all awry and sitting, sulking)

GENERAL: (Noting that his ruse is working, as his daughters are now free, and rubbing it in.) I ask you, have you ever known what it is to be an oooorphan? (He straightens the King's hat)

KING: Often! (Grabbing his hat and messing it back up, out of spite.)

DIRECTOR: That was awesome. The whole hat bit, it just developed out of the emotions. When you let the emotions out, move, and use your props and costumes, you discover great things from your heart. But I don't want to you to fixate on the hat bit in future rehearsals of this scene. Continue to be creative, and in the moment, and responding to each other, and using props. Good things will happen. Keep the hat bit if you want, but stay free to discover. And General, I loved how you taunted him, I've never seen anyone do it that way before, and it is so refreshing. Keep rubbing it in, and see where that goes.

GENERAL: (leaning down, toward King's ear) Yes, ooooorphan. Have you ever known what it is to be one?

KING: (Yelling in anguish) I say, often.

PIRATES: (disgusted) Often, often, often. (Turning away)

DIRECTOR: Pirates, what are you feeling? Because that reaction sounded like you were unsure.

PIRATE 1. Well, we're going to lose another battle, and this one had a woman as the booty, so I'm pretty disappointed.

PIRATE 2. The General is now winning. That disgusts me.

PIRATE 3. And our King is as weak as I am.

DIRECTOR: Let's try something. You repeat the same word three times, right? Each of you create a angular gesture that expresses your feelings. Three moves. One for each word. Make each one bigger than the one before. Like this, Pow, POW, **POW!**

PIRATES: Often, OFTEN, **OFTEN!**

DIRECTOR: Great. I like it. Except you are all now so strong in the give and take, that if you freeze this way, I don't know if we'll even hear the next dialog, as we'll all be focused on you, your energy. So, for the sake of focus we need to weaken you. So, do it again, just like that, or with any new three moves you want, but after you do the third, sag and weaken yourselves into a tableau of disappointment you can hold. Some of you might form a tight group with the unifying emotion of disappointment. Go!

PIRATES: Often, OFTEN, **OFTEN!** (They create powerful

moves on each word, then collapse into weaker positions and groups.)

DIRECTOR: Great. Continue.

GENERAL: I don't think we quite understand one another. I ask you, have you ever known what it is to be an orphan, and you say "orphan". As I understand you, you are merely repeating the word "orphan" to show that you understand me.

KING: I didn't repeat the word often.

GENERAL: Pardon me, you did indeed.

KING: (Jumping to his feet) I only repeated it once. (face to face with General)

GENERAL: True, but you repeated it.

KING: But not often.

GENERAL: Stop! I think I see where we are getting confused. When you said "orphan", did you mean "orphan" – a person who has lost his parents, or "often", frequently?

KING: Ah! I beg pardon – I see what you mean – frequently.

GENERAL: Ah! you said "often", frequently.

KING: No, only once.

GENERAL: (irritated) Exactly – you said "often", frequently, only once.

DIRECTOR: OK, I let that dialog go to the end of the scene to see what you would naturally do with it. It's a witty scene, wordplay games, and you did it well, just standing there and sorting out the use of "often" versus "orphan." Its a bit arcane. But audiences deserve to hear it.

One thing we need to do is build the pace toward the beat. The beat in this scene is about as clear as I've ever seen in any dialog because at the peak General yells Stop! So, that's a great place to stop. So, when you do it again from "Often, Often Often," build the pace and the intensity up to the word, "Stop." Then start building again to the end of the scene.

Another thing we have to do is find the subtext that makes this arcane wordplay intriguing, and as always, the secret is in your character and the situation. So lets think about that. General, you just sang a self-introduction that bragged about yourself. What does that tell us about your character that we could work with. I ask that of everyone. What is his character that could apply to this wordplay? (lots of discussion follows...leading to)

DAUGHTER 1: He loves wordplay. The whole thing about finding a rhyme for "strategy" was fun for him.

DAUGHTER 2: He would be the kind of guy who plays scrabble every night.

PIRATE 1: Does crossword puzzles.

PIRATE 2: And keeps score, times himself, knows his personal record.

DIRECTOR: So, he is in his element, and he is compelled to sort through this confusion of words. He can't give up. He is obsessive about getting the words right.

So what about King? What is his character regarding this. I'm asking everybody. (lots of discussion ...leading to)

PIRATE 1. He is definitely NOT interested in words. He is a man of action. He wins battles, not word games.

DAUGHTER 1. So, he doesn't even engage. He's not interested in solving the misunderstanding.

DIRECTOR: OK, lets do that again, this time, build the pace to "Stop," then build again til the end. Let the emotions play out as General gets excited about solving the misunderstanding, and King gets totally annoyed. Let these emotions motivate approach avoidance, and remember to give and take.

DISCUSSION: This example would be one part of the rehearsal sequence. After working though the scene, we would repeat the scene a few more times, each with less and less interruption by the director. We would still encourage characters to discover and react to each other. There is still much that has not yet been discovered. There are refinements that will happen as the rehearsals progress.

For example, in a later rehearsal the director might notice that the character of Major General has become more of a buffoon than he would like. In which case, rather than undoing the work that has been done, he would simply ask the General to still feel the urges to do all the things he's practiced but to stifle them behind a sophisticated, studied, and well-manner exterior. That layer of Inner-Adult self-control would be struggling to manage the raw Inner-Child emotions he is carrying. That struggle, self-control versus emotional explosions, would enrich the scene in a manner that would be quite dynamic.

As the show approaches, actors will naturally settle into very predictable blocking. They will know what to expect from each other. The scene will set itself, like a stream that bubbles down the hillside then eventually settles into a calm lake, or like concrete that tumbles in a mixer, pours into a mold, then hardens over time.

Final Words of Advice.

When you rehearse scenes it is OK if you do not know all the right questions to ask. In fact, as a director who has a day job and wants to keep it, there may be scenes you are not very sure about. Don't worry. I've done *Pirates of Penzance* a bunch of times, so this scene is familiar to me. Don't be intimidated.

Instead, remember the skills you have taught in workshops.

1. Coach your actors to move, using all the common crosses, body positions, and stage positions.

2. Teach them to give and take.

3. Coach them to approach or avoid.

4. Remind them to balance the stage.

5. Ask them their objectives. Ask them how they feel. Ask them to struggle with their choices.

6. Ask them to hold the tableau.

7. When you have groups on stage, remind them to take their own space, or to form groups.

Those simple reminders will yield an awesome show. Relax and go for it. Enjoy the art of directing.

And keep it stress free.

Buy the Companion Book in the *Stress Free Theater* series *Coaching Pre-Broadway Actors* by
Daniel B. Mills

Author, Daniel B. Mills, earned a degree in theater education from the University of Southern Maine, and two graduate degrees from the University of Maine. He worked his day job as an English teacher, then as a school counselor, and adult education director. He is a retired high school principal.

Over the years, he directed over 200 shows, and that includes loosing count about 20 years ago. He founded the Ice Cream Theater for Children, the SandCastle Children's Theater, and the Children's Theater of the Island Arts Festival. He co-founded the Maine Music Theater, and coached dramatic arts in high schools in Maine. His high schools entered the Maine Drama Festival 9 times, and were awarded 6 trips to the state finals, and 3 to the New Englands. His directing style was always creative and spirited, and he loved to create beautiful stage pictures, feeling that theater is the ultimate social art form.

He performed as a solo artist doing children's entertainment with magic, juggling, mime, and story telling. During his youth and college years he was a folksinger, and was musical director for a USO tour.

He has performed in all of the Gilbert and Sullivan Operas, and several of them more than once. He was the lead comic actor in the 1994 International Gilbert and Sullivan Festival in Buxton England when his company won the International Trophy.

Dan is a resident of Florida but lives in the summer in Bar Harbor, Maine, the home of Acadia National Park where he sails, canoes, hikes, and helps his wife, Joan, operate lodging businesses.

His largest audience was when he performed as the narrator, playing a dozen different roles, in *L'Histoire du Soldat*, by Stravinsky with the Bangor Symphony Orchestra at a concert by the jam band Phish, before 70,000 Phish Phans.

Dan and Joan raised five sons, all of whom are theater fans, including one who is a Broadway actor, one who is a movie animator, one who is a middle school theater director, another who is a swing dancer in Manhattan where he owns his own small business, and one who won a play writing contest at Dartmouth and is now the father of four children of his own. There is a legacy of theater in the Mills family that may extend a few more generations.

Alphabetical Index

Absenteeism......................100
Acting Workshops...............51
Actors as Creative Geniuses 97
Advantage 1. No Pre-Blocking............................105
Advantage 2. Creative Input 106
Advantage 3. Actors Develop Problem Solving Skill.......106
Advantage 4. Motivation is Inherent..............................108
Advantage 5. Comfort on Stage....................................110
Advantage 6. Characters are More Believable.................110
Advantage 7. Replacement Actors Fit in Quickly..........111
Advantage 8. Less Stress for the Director and Cast.........112
Affirm Your Actors as they Take Risks.........................22
Anxious hunter finds the missing person....................167
Applaud Every Report-Out. 53
Approach-Avoid.................198
Approach-Avoidance...51, 180
Array...................................133
Arrayed in Groups..............134
Arrayed in Lines.................133
Arrayed in Open Spacing. .135
Assign Important Tasks to Your Mixed Teams...............50
Assign Some Rehearsal Time to Scene Teams....................35
Asymmetrical.....................132
Avoid being Controlling 59
Avoid Parallel Crosses.......158

Back Away Then Turn to Run 190, 201, 257
Balance the Stage..........67, 80
Be a Post-Modern Leader....20
Business-as-Usual..............168
Center Balance....................70
Center of Gravity.................69
Chance encounter..............165
Character Tableau 204
Circular Balance...................75
Composition Pitfalls............65
Composition in Art.............82
Control the Visual Focus.....84
Convince Someone............188
Counter...............................156
Create Focus......................117
Cross...........................148, 261
Cross and Pivot..................153
Cross Away 152
Cross in Front....................150
Cross To 151
Cross Upstage....................154
Desire to Escape a Situation 189
Desire to Escape a Thought 190
Development of Free Blocking..............................86

295

Dynamic Composition through Side-Coaching......245
Eight Parameters of Tight Groups..............................212
Encourage Movement........263
Escape a Situation. 201
Escape a Thought..............201
Exit Line...........................164
Face Away........................144
Fixing the Semi-Circles ...242
Flat Balance........................69
Flow.................................239
Form Tight Groups............212
Free Blocking.....................90
Freeze the Feet of the High Status Character.................259
Full Stage Tableau.............205
Get the Feet Moving..........259
Give and Take......51, 174, 179
Give Away the Directing 29
Groups..............................210
Hopeful lovers...................167
Invite a Dream Team...........30
Lead with the Chest...........255
Lead with the Head...........255
Lead with the Wrist...........256
Learn actor's names............22
Levels...............................128
Manifest the Relationships 237
Meaningful Movements:...252
Movement.........................147
One Character Moves at a Time.................................158
Off-Center..........................73
Offer Applause....................23
Offer Appreciation..............45

Open Up............................153
Organize the Rehearsals......26
Pivot.................................145
Project Energy From Your Core Out Through Your Fingertips 256
Put the Struggler in the Middle...............................253
Traditional Blocking...........87
Reach Out and Touch Someone...........................252
Rehearsals........................120
Relate...............................262
Relate 193
Relative Strength of Body Position 124, 126
Report-Outs........................52
Review the Choreography...51
Rhythm 191
Roller-Coaster....................74
Rounds on a Prop................50
Run 261
Sample Scene....................269
Scene Teams.......................35
Select Project Leaders Randomly...........................51
Sense of urgency...............186
Sequenced Freezes............161
Set Up..............................169
Setting the Scene...............241
Share a vision 33
Share the thanks.................23
Sharing.............................146
Short Run with Motivated Stop.................................200
Short Runs 185

Side-Coach 114
Slow Reveal or Quick Reveal
.... 258
Solving Common Staging
Problems............................ 242
Status Work.......................... 51
Stock Blocking Patterns.... 162
Stop on the Stairs............... 209
Stop Yourself from Running
Away.................................... 257
Struggle with That............. 199
Subtext............................... 197
Subtextual Phrases that
Motivate Avoidance........... 183
Sweeping Turns................. 157
Swing Balance..................... 74
Swing Your Face Toward the
Audience............................ 163
Teach Actors to Create
Beautiful Tableaux............. 122
Teach Actors to Move........ 118
Teach Actors to Take Their
Own Space......................... 115
Teach the Ensemble to Flow
.... 240
Thank individuals, often...... 23
The Director as Leader 18
The Director as Teacher....... 13
The Principles of Free
Blocking............................. 113

Think in Static Pictures 208
Thrill.......................... 187, 200
Tight Groups................ 51, 212
Tone................................... 192
Triangles.............................. 78
Trouble-Shoot...................... 41
True Story about the Power of
Relating.............................. 195
True Story about a Bad
Decision I Made................. 103
True Story about A
Catastrophe Avoided............ 92
True Story About an Actor's
Idea 98
True Story about the Power of
Applause.............................. 23
True Story of A Scene Team 38
True Story of Jackson, the
Backstage Bear..................... 46
True Story of the ATV......... 55
True Story of the Harp......... 55
Trust the Process................ 266
Turn.................................... 153
Unwitting introduction...... 166
Urgency.............................. 201
Use Humorous Methods to
Randomly Mix Your Teams. 49
Variety and Unity................. 84
Scene teams......................... 51

Made in the USA
Middletown, DE
08 December 2019